(

MW01196446

Manifesting His Beauty and Displaying His Worth

1

In Love with

Christ

The Narrative of *Sarah Edwards*

Edited and Annotated by Jennifer Adams

In Love with Christ: The Narrative of Sarah Edwards

is the collective edition of

*Her Uncommon Discoveries of the Divine Perfections and Glory;
And of the Excellency of Christ*
by Sarah Pierrepont Edwards (1710-1758) in
*The Works of President Edwards:
With a Memoir of His Life* by Sereno Edwards Dwight
Originally published by G. & C. & H. Carvill
New York, 1830

and

"Thoughts on the Revival" section V. by Jonathan Edwards in
The Works of Jonathan Edwards, Vol. 1 Published in 1834, Great Britain

This collective, grammatically updated edition with additional material is published by

CORNER PILLAR PRESS

"Let our daughters be as corner pillars,
Fashioned as for a palace."
Psalm 144:12

Forest, VA
Copyright © 2010 Jennifer Adams
All rights reserved
Printed in the United States of America

ISBN: 978-0-9844320-1-1

cornerpillarpress@gmail.com
www.cornerpillarpress.com

Edited and Typeset by
Jennifer Adams

Front Cover: Sarah Edwards

4

Dedicated to My Four Corner Pillars

Mary Bethany
Elisabeth Victoria
Sarah Kate
Anna Grace

May the Lord grace each of you with an
"Uncommon union" like Jonathan and Sarah;
And to my little Sarah Kate in particular:
May the Lord make you a true "daughter of Sarah,"
Fulfilling your name's sake after Sarah of the Bible,
Sarah Edwards, and Kate Luther.

Other Books by Corner Pillar Press:

Completer to a Contender for the Faith Series
A Basket of Summer Fruit, by Susannah Spurgeon
Ann Judson: Missionary Wife,
Volume I of The Lives of the Three Mrs. Judsons by Arabella Stuart
Edited, expanded, and revised by Jennifer Adams
Delighting in Her Heavenly Bridegroom:
The Memoirs of Harriet Newell, Teenage Missionary Wife
Edited and annotated by Jennifer Adams
Following Her Beloved: The Memoirs of Henrietta Shuck,
Missionary Wife and Mother
Compiled by Jeremiah Jeter; edited by Jennifer Adams
With Cords of Love: The Memoirs of Elizabeth Dwight,
Missionary Wife and Mother
Compiled by Harrison Dwight; edited by Jennifer Adams

Puritan Works
Preparation for Suffering, John Flavel
The Fountain of Life: A Display of Christ in His Essential
and Mediatorial Glory, John Flavel
The Return of Prayers: Sowing Seeds of Prayer and
Waiting on God for a Harvest of Answers, by Thomas Goodwin
Importunity: Refusing to Give Up in Prayer, by Christopher Love
Faith in Prayer, by David Clarkson

Contents

Preface to the Series

In Love with Christ: The Narrative of Sarah Edwards is the second book in the "Completer to a Contender for the Faith" series.[1] These books are published to cast a vision for our daughters of godliness, faithfulness, and biblical femininity. Each of these books focuses on a woman in history who has impacted the world for Christ, with a special emphasis on her role as a completer to a "contender for the faith." This phrase comes from Jude 1:3 which says, "I felt the necessity to write to you appealing that you *contend earnestly for the faith* which was once for all delivered to the saints." Throughout church history, God has raised up men to contend for the truth of the gospel. The faithfulness of their wives to encourage them to "fight the good fight"[2] and "finish the course"[3] is worth studying and imitating.

In the "Completer to a Contender for the Faith" series, we seek to publish the original writings of such women or any other first-hand material concerning them. It is no exaggeration to say that many of the men whom God has used throughout church history have fulfilled their ministry, in large part, due to the prayers, encouragement, and sacrifice of their wives. Without this important but often unseen ministry, the church today might not

---

[1] The first book is *A Basket of Summer Fruit,* by Susannah Spurgeon, also published by Corner Pillar Press. The other books include *Ann Judson: Missionary Wife,* by Arabella Stuart—revised, edited, and expanded by Jennifer Adams; *Delighting in Her Heavenly Bridegroom: The Memoirs of Harriet Newell, Teenage Missionary Wife* edited and annotated by Jennifer Adams; *Following Her Beloved: The Memoirs of Henrietta Shuck, Missionary Wife and Mother,* compiled by Jeremiah Jeter, edited and expanded by Jennifer Adams; and *With Cords of Love: The Memoirs of Elizabeth Dwight, Missionary Wife and Mother* compiled by Harrison Dwight, edited by Jennifer Adams.
[2] II Timothy 4:7
[3] Ibid.

be standing quite as high on the shoulders of those who have gone before.

There are several predominant themes that run parallel in the lives of these women: 1) they each had their own relationship with Christ, independent of their husbands, from which they drew their strength; 2) they were intellectually strong, theologically like-minded, and of a kindred spirit with their husbands; 3) they shared a sweet spiritual union with their husbands that fortified their men to face the meanest foe and graced them to enjoy God's presence together before the throne in a way they never could alone; 4) they believed one of the best ways they could serve God was to allow Him to cut and fashion them into the "velvet steel" upon which their husbands could lean; 5) they embraced their husbands' vision and ministry fully, and gave of themselves not only to their husbands and children but also to the church and the spread of the gospel; 6) there came a point in their husbands' lives when they faced large-scale persecution due to contending for the faith. These women joined their husbands in "not [being] ashamed of the gospel"[4] by partaking in "the fellowship of His sufferings."[5] As a result, the gospel advanced through their husbands' ministries, across international borders, and down through the generations—even to this day.

These women were not perfect. They had struggles and weaknesses—but they each counted Christ and His gospel worthy of their lives. For this reason, they go down in history as women whom we want to emulate. Our prayer is that as we study the lives of these women, our daughters will embrace a vision for the ministry of being a "completer to a contender for the faith." Furthermore, we pray that our daughters will be pointed to the

---

[4] Romans 1:16
[5] Philippians 3:10

fountainhead of love and strength from which these women drew—the Lord Jesus Christ

Preface to the Book

The narrative of Sarah Edwards was originally recorded by Sarah as a testimony to the work of God in her life. After reading her testimony, her husband decided to publish it. However, in order to protect it from being misconstrued, he rewrote it in the third person. In doing so, he omitted many personal details. Nevertheless, the sweetness of Jonathan's heart and mind come through in his rendition, making it a different yet worthwhile read. In modern terms, Jonathan's edition of Sarah's narrative was written through "Edwardian" theological glasses. Therefore, there are two editions of the narrative of Sarah Edwards—one by Sarah herself, and one by her husband, Jonathan.

The grandson of Jonathan and Sarah Edwards, Sereno Edwards Dwight, later published the works of his grandfather in a ten volume set entitled *The Works of President Edwards.*[6] He included the narrative of Sarah in his works. However, he used Sarah's original first-person manuscript rather than Jonathan's third person manuscript, which is the one most commonly read today. This edition of Sarah's narrative entitled *In Love with Christ: The Narrative of Sarah Edwards* is a collective, grammatically updated edition containing *both* manuscripts. The essence of the two narratives is the same, but the manner in which they are presented is strikingly different. Each one is equally breathtaking, convicting, and spiritually exhilarating.

For ease of reading, some of the gender neutral references in Jonathan's edition have been changed to the feminine form. Long sentences have been broken in two. Otherwise, the texts have

---

[6] Jonathan Edwards was the president of the College of New Jersey, which is now Princeton University.

been preserved in their original condition, and every effort has been made to retain the beauty, meaning, and feel of the original language. Special thanks to Mary Bethany Adams, Cheryl Nester, and Sue Palmer for proofreading the prefaces and introductions, and to Bethany Joshua and Courtney Joshua for proof-reading the entire manuscript.

Finally, since this book is published primarily for daughters (although everyone, young and old, male and female, is encouraged to read it[7]) we have included the testimony of God's grace during the Great Awakening upon a four-year-old girl named Phebe, with an introduction by my daughter, Mary Bethany. May the Lord visit us, *and our daughters*, once again with His infinite love and inexpressible grace! To Him be the glory!

---

[7] This may be one of the reasons why Jonathan originally published it in the third person gender neutral.

Foreword

In speaking of Mrs. Edwards, we have already had occasion to remark that her piety appears to have been in no ordinary degree pure, intense, and elevated, and her views of spiritual and heavenly things were uncommonly clear and joyful. Near the close of the year 1738, according to the testimony of Mr. Edwards, she was led in an uncommon discovery of God's excellency and of a high exercise of love to Him. She was graced to make a new and most solemn dedication of herself to God, His service, and His glory, as well as an entire renunciation of the world. After this, she often had such views of the glory of the divine perfections and of Christ's excellencies that she was overwhelmed, and as it were, swallowed up in the light and joy of the love of God. In the summer of 1740, after a new and more perfect resignation of herself to God, with yet greater fervency, her views of the glory of God and of the excellency of Christ became still more clear and transporting. In the following winter, after a similar, but more perfect resignation of herself and acceptance of God as the only portion and happiness of her soul, God appeared to vouchsafe to her a degree of spiritual light and enjoyment which seemed to be, in reality, an anticipation of the joys of the heavenly world. There was so much that was unusual and striking in this state of mind that her husband requested her to draw up an exact statement of it, which, having been preserved, is now presented to the reader.

Sereno Edwards Dwight
Grandson of Jonathan and Sarah Edwards
The Works of President Edwards. With a Memoir of His Life,
New York, 1830

Section I

Introduction to Sarah Edwards

Sarah was the wife of America's greatest theologian, Jonathan Edwards. It was through the preaching of her husband[8] that the Lord "visited"[9] the people of the American colonies and brought about what has become known as the First Great Awakening.

An awakening is a divine outpouring of God's Spirit upon a collective people over a large geographical area that produces multiple conversions, deeper levels of conviction, hatred of sin, comprehensive repentance, corporate consecration, complete resignation, delight in God's law, and greater heights of love to God. This is due to a resplendent unveiling of God, His glory, His attributes, and His love made manifest in Christ crucified. The cumulative result of an awakening is an all-consuming love for God, His Son, His Spirit, His glory, His church, and the spread of the gospel among the unconverted, that they might share in the same joy and happiness of being united to Christ through faith, so God's glory might fill the earth as the waters cover the sea.[10]

The First Great Awakening swept over both sides of the Atlantic in the 1730's and 1740's. It covered the American colonies, and not only produced individual and ecclesiastical changes, but laid the groundwork for the establishment of a Christian Republic now known as the United States of America.

---

[8] As well as others, such as George Whitefield and Samuel Davies, to name a few.

[9] When the Lord "visits" His people, He manifests His presence in an unusual way to bless His people and/or judge unrepentant sinners. See Gen. 21:1; 50:24-25; Ex. 3:16; 4:31; 32:24; 34:7; Lev. 18:25; Deut. 5:9; Ruth 1:6; I Sam. 2:21; Ps. 89:32; 106:4; Jer. 29:10; Luke 1:78; 7:16; 19:44; I Pet. 2:12.

[10] Hab. 2:14

17

Moreover, it moved the people with great concern for the African slaves. The eyes of men were opened to the urgent need to bring them the gospel, teach them to read, and abolish slavery.[11]

An awakening is a work of God alone, "who is in the heavens and who does whatever He pleases."[12] However, there are means of grace God has given to usher in the outpouring of His Spirit. While Jonathan Edwards was a "sinner saved by grace" like the rest of us, he employed the means of grace in an unrelenting manner. As a result, God was pleased to reveal Himself[13] with a similar intensity that was comprehensive, pervasive, and transforming—for Jonathan and Sarah, their church, and the American colonies. Furthermore, in light of Jonathan's published works, which are read and studied by many today, it may be no exaggeration to say—for the world.

What are the means of grace Jonathan so vigorously pursued? They are prayer, the study of the Word, covenant love for the church, corporate worship, a fierce forsaking of sin, a renouncing of the things of this world, a determination to have God whatever the cost, and a radically disciplined life lived moment-by-moment in pursuit of the sweet, satisfying presence of God.

The Seedling of the Great Awakening

Sarah was born on January 9, 1710, in New Haven, Connecticut to a distinguished family. She was raised in the Christian faith and sat under the preaching of her father, Rev. James Pierrepont. As a pastor, her father played a significant role in the establishment of Yale College.[14] This fact proved providential in bringing Jonathan

---

[11] Jonathan Edwards' son, Jonathan, was instrumental in speaking out against slavery.
[12] Psalm 115:3
[13] See James 4:8; II Chronicles 15:2; Hosea 6:3
[14] Now known as Yale University

and Sarah together. When Jonathan was nineteen, he took a teaching position at Yale and attended Sarah's church. On the front page of his grammar book, Jonathan made this observation of Sarah when she was only thirteen:

They say there is a young lady in New Haven who is beloved of the Great Being who made and rules the world, and that there are certain seasons in which this Great Being, in some way or other invisible, comes to her and fills her mind with exceeding sweet delight, and that she hardly cares for anything except to meditate on Him; that she expects after a while to be received up where He is, to be raised up out of the world and caught up into heaven, being assured that He loves her too well to let her remain at a distance from Him always. There she is to dwell with Him and to be ravished with His love and delight forever. Therefore, if you present all the world before her with the richest of its treasures she disregards it and cares not for it and is unmindful of any pain or affliction. She has a strange sweetness in her mind and singular purity in her affections, is most just and conscientious in all her conduct; and you could not persuade her to do anything wrong or sinful if you would give her all the world, lest she should offend this Great Being. She is of a wonderful sweetness, calmness, and universal benevolence of mind, especially after this Great God has manifested Himself to her mind. She will sometimes go about from place to place, singing sweetly; and seems to be always full of joy and pleasure, and no one knows for what. She loves to be alone, walking in the fields and groves, and seems to have someone invisible always conversing with her.[15]

---

[15] Jonathan Edwards. *The Works of Jonathan Edwards,* Vol. 1 (Peabody, MA: Hendrickson, 1998), lxxxi.

The portrait Jonathan painted of Sarah depicts the seedlings of her own awakening and the beginnings of the First Great Awakening. However, while Jonathan was contemplating a courtship with Sarah, there was another courtship in motion. There was another who was wooing her—one more powerful, more beautiful, more irresistible than any other—it was the Lord Jesus Christ. This is why Jonathan was captivated by her— because he, too, was the object of God's love pursuit. Just as Jonathan, the son of Saul, felt his soul instantly "knit" to David because of their mutual love for the Lord, so Jonathan Edwards felt his soul inextricably linked to Sarah. From that moment on, it was clear that Jonathan and Sarah, who were deeply in love with Christ, would be in love with each other. They could do none other than delight in the fruit of the Spirit they "tasted" in each other and bask in the shared love they had for Christ, finding their greatest joy in worshiping Him together. Jonathan's marriage proposal to Sarah might have been, "O magnify the Lord with me, and let us exalt His name together!"[16] Likewise, she might have replied, "We will rejoice in You [O Lord] and be glad. We will extol Your love more than wine."[17] Such intense passion for Christ and commitment to His glory are rare among His people. It is even more uncommon to observe this depth of love and devotion in two young people among the same congregation. Wed those two people together, and you most certainly have an "uncommon union"[18] and the beginnings of a Great Awakening!

---

[16] Psalm 34:3

[17] Song of Solomon 1:4

[18] This is the term Jonathan used to describe his life-long relationship with his wife, Sarah.

Faithful Wife

Jonathan and Sarah married July 28, 1727, four years after he first fell in love with the young lady who was the beloved of the Lord. Jonathan had just become the pastor of his grandfather's prestigious church in Northampton. Every morning, before sunrise, Jonathan woke up the entire household for worship. He routinely read a chapter from the Bible by candlelight and allotted the rest of the time to prayer. Jonathan spent the next ten hours seeking the Lord, writing treatises, and preparing sermons. Sarah often visited him in his study. What a pleasure it must have been to converse with her over the meaning of a certain verse, seek her counsel, or simply share sweet fellowship with her. In the late afternoon, Jonathan provided academic instruction for his daughters and shared the evening meal with his family. Afterward, he spent an hour engaging his children in pleasant conversation, singing, and Bible instruction. He retired to his study for another two to three hours before bedtime, closing the evening in prayer with his beloved wife, Sarah.

Sarah fulfilled her role as wife and mother with utmost devotion and grace. She was a faithful mother to eleven children[19] and responsible for a large portion of their discipline and instruction. In addition, her heart and home were always open to hospitality, as she regularly received traveling guests and pastoral apprentices. One guest, the Rev. George Whitefield, made this observation regarding Sarah:

> She was a woman adorned with a meek and quiet spirit, talked feelingly and solidly of the things of God, and seemed to be such a helpmate for her husband that she caused me to renew

---

[19] A twelfth child was born and died in infancy.

those prayers, which for many months I have put up to God, that He would be pleased to send me a daughter of Abraham to be my wife.[20]

Another guest, Samuel Hopkins,[21] made this observation of Jonathan and Sarah while staying in their home for several months:

He [Jonathan] found at home one who was in every sense a helpmeet for him; one who made their common dwelling the abode of order and neatness, of peace and comfort, of harmony and love to all its inmates, and of kindness and hospitality to the friend, the visitor, and the stranger. While [Sarah] uniformly paid a becoming deference to her husband and treated him with entire respect, she spared no pains in conforming to his inclination and rendering everything in the family agreeable and pleasant; accounting it her greatest glory and *there wherein she could best serve God and her generation* to be the means in this way of promoting his usefulness and happiness. . . . No person of discernment could be conversant in the family without observing and admiring the perfect harmony, mutual love, and esteem that subsisted between them . . . It was a happy circumstance that he [Jonathan] could trust everything . . . to the care of Mrs. Edwards with entire safety and with undoubting confidence. She was a most judicious and faithful mistress of the family, habitually industrious, a sound

---

[20] Noel Piper, *Faithful Women and Their Extraordinary God* (Wheaton, Ill: Crossway Publishers, 2005), 27 quoting Ola Winslow, *Jonathan Edwards: 1703-1758: A Biography* (New York: Macmillan, 1940), 188.
[21] Samuel Hopkins stayed in the Edwards home for eight months, during which he apprenticed for the ministry under Jonathan. Shortly after Jonathan's death, Hopkins wrote a biography on the life of Jonathan Edwards, providing first-hand accounts of his preaching, character, and family.

economist, managing her household affairs with diligence and discretion. [22]

Hopkins continued with describing a typical day in the Edwards' household. He wrote:

[Jonathan] maintained a great esteem and regard for his amiable and excellent consort. [23] Much tenderness and kindness were expressed in his conversation with her and conduct towards her. He was wont frequently to admit her into his study and converse freely with her on matters of religion, and he used to commonly pray with her in his study at least once a day unless something extraordinary prevented. The time in which this used to be commonly attended was just before going to bed after family prayers. As he rose very early himself, he was wont to have his family up in the morning; after which, before the family entered the business of the day, he attended on family prayers; a chapter in the Bible was read commonly by candle-light in the winter; upon which he asked his children questions according to their age and capacity; and took occasion to explain some passages in it or enforce any duty recommended as he thought most proper.

He took many pains to instruct them in the principles of religion; in which he made use of the Westminster Shorter Catechism, not merely by taking care that they learned it by heart, but by leading them into an understanding of the doctrines therein taught, by asking them questions on each answer and explaining it to them. His usual time to attend this was the evening before the Sabbath. And, as he believed that

---

[22] *The Works of Jonathan Edwards,* Vol. 1: lxxxvii.
[23] wife

the Sabbath, or holy time, began at sunset the evening before the day, he ordered his family to finish all their secular business by that time or before; whence they were all called together, and a psalm was sung and prayer attended as an introduction to sanctifying the Sabbath. This care and exactness effectually prevented the intruding on holy time by attending to secular business, [which is] too common in families where the evening before the Sabbath is pretended to be observed. He was a great enemy to young people's unseasonable company keeping and frolicking, as he looked upon it as a great means of corrupting and ruining youth. . . He did not allow his children to be [away] from home after nine o'clock at night . . . and neither were they allowed to stay up much after that time in his own house when any came to visit them. If any gentleman desired acquaintance with his daughters, after handsomely introducing himself by properly consulting the parents, he was allowed all proper opportunity for it, and a room and fire if needed; but must not intrude on the proper hours of rest and sleep, nor the religion and order of the family.[24]

Jonathan and Sarah ordered their entire household around the Lord, His Word, and His church. Sarah viewed her role of helpmate as her "spiritual ministry" to the Lord. She wisely understood that in doing all she could to minister to her husband by keeping their home pleasant and productive, she was freeing him to do what God had called him to do—pray, study, write, and preach. She recognized that she would rightly share in the spiritual rewards he would later receive. She encapsulated the definition of

[24] Samuel Hopkins. *The Life and Character of the Late Reverend, Learned, and Pious Mr. Jonathan Edwards* (Northampton, MA: Andrew Wright, 1804), 46-48.

being a "completer to a contender for the faith," in that she whole-heartedly embraced her call and the sacrifices that came with it. As a result, there could not have been a holier, more intimate marriage on earth. For this reason, upon his deathbed, Jonathan spoke these words concerning his beloved wife of twenty-nine years:

> Give my kindest love to my dear wife, and tell her, that the *uncommon union*, which has so long subsisted between us, has been of such a nature, as I trust is spiritual, and therefore will continue forever.[25]

The union between Jonathan and Sarah was indeed "uncommon," not only because Sarah was his devoted wife in the ministry, but because *both* Jonathan and Sarah drank deeply from the immeasurable love of God in Christ. They both panted *relentlessly* after God. They both rid themselves of sin and everything that stood in the way of having, knowing, and loving Christ. They both counted *everything* as loss compared to the surpassing value of knowing Christ Jesus.[26]

What happens when two people, who are deeply in love with Christ, are joined together not only in the one-flesh union of marriage but also in a kindred-spirit union by His Spirit? An explosion of love, rapturous joy, holy communion, and a ministry that continues to bear fruit *hundreds* of years after their deaths for the glory of God—all over the world!

---

[25] Sereno Edwards Dwight, "Memoirs of Jonathan Edwards," in *The Works of Jonathan Edwards,* Vol. 1: clxxvii.
[26] Philippians 3:8

Fruitful Mother

The fruitfulness of Jonathan and Sarah's union was abundant, extensive, and glorious. Their children possessed the same devotion to Christ and sweet spirit that marked their parents. Not only did all of their children love the Lord, but many of their grandchildren and great-grandchildren did as well. By the year 1900, there were over 100 Edwards descendants serving as pastors, missionaries, and mission board trustees. In addition, there were 13 college presidents, 65 professors, 100 lawyers, 30 judges, 66 physicians, 60 authors, and 80 men who held public office. This was only 143 years after their deaths! We do not have a record of the on-going fruit to this day, but we imagine that it is staggering.

While many of the Edwards descendants trace their heritage to their renowned grandfather, there is no doubt that Sarah's influence upon their children, especially their eight daughters, carried the greatest weight. Sons imitate their fathers, but daughters imitate their mothers. Although Jonathan blessed his daughters with a biblical foundation and developed their intellects for the glory of God, it most likely was Sarah who shaped their character.

It is interesting to note that the Edwards household was predominately female. This is surprising. One would think that Jonathan would have been given many sons to train for the ministry—but in the providence of God, it was Sarah who was given many daughters to establish a multi-generational lineage of faithfulness! Sarah raised mature, Christ-like daughters who were competent, compassionate, and full of grace. They reflected her deep-seated love for Christ and embraced Him fully as their own. The following eulogy, spoken in honor of her daughter, Esther, testifies to Sarah's legacy:

Mrs. Esther Edwards Burr exceeded most women in the beauty of her person, as well as in her behavior and conversation. She discovered an unaffected, natural freedom towards persons of all ranks with whom she conversed. Her genius was much more than common. She had a lively, sprightly imagination, a quick and penetrating discernment, and a good judgment. She possessed an uncommon degree of wit and vivacity; which yet was consistent with pleasantness and good nature; and she knew how to be facetious and sportive, without trespassing on the bounds of decorum or of strict and serious religion. In short, she seemed formed to please, and especially to please one of Mr. Burr's taste and character, in whom she was exceedingly happy. But what crowned all her excellencies and was her chief glory was *religion*. She appeared to be the subject of divine impressions when seven or eight years old; and she made a public profession of religion when about fifteen. Her conversation until her death was exemplary, as becometh godliness[27]—she was, in every respect, an ornament to her sex, being equally distinguished for the suavity of her manners, her literary accomplishments, and her unfeigned regard to religion. Her religion did not cast a gloom over her mind, but made her cheerful and happy, and rendered the thought of death transporting. She left a number of manuscripts on interesting subjects, and it was hoped they would have been made public, but they are now lost.[28]

Biographer Elisabeth D. Dodds noted, "Many men found the Edwards daughters to be exceptionally attractive."[29] It might have

---

[27] I Timothy 2:10

[28] *The Works of Jonathan Edwards* vol. 1: ccxxi.

[29] Elisabeth D Dodds. *Marriage a Difficult Man*, (Laurel, MO: Audubon Press, 2003), 33, 43.

been a physical attraction, but in light of the spiritual attraction their mother possessed, it most likely was something far deeper than skin. Like their mother, they radiated the love of Christ, and it was probably the warmth of His love that drew men.

The emphasis of Sarah's influence upon their character is not meant to diminish the impact of Jonathan. In fact, he personally tutored his daughters in Greek, Latin, rhetoric, penmanship, history, and geography, not to mention the Bible, church history, and hermeneutics.[29] This is significant because daughters were rarely educated beyond reading, writing, and arithmetic in those days. For this reason, Jonathan made sure that while his sons studied at school,[30] his daughters were learning at home. His daughters grew up to have a reputation for being "highly intellectual" with a "voracious appetite for reading" and "striking mental traits, quick habits of observation, and a thorough keen analysis of men and events."[31] While Sarah's motherly influence can never be overestimated, Jonathan was also a faithful father who gave his daughters the priceless gift of knowledge.

The fruitfulness of Jonathan and Sarah does not stop at their family tree. It transcends bloodlines and extends to multiple generations all over the world. Countless men and women have been profoundly impacted through the writings of Jonathan Edwards. Only eternity will reveal the far-reaching extent he has had through his published works and the innumerable spiritual

---

[29] Elisabeth D. Dodds, *Marriage to a Difficult Man,* 41, 124.
[30] In 1694, Jonathan's father, Timothy Edwards, was the school master of Northampton. By 1725, Dr. Samuel Mather and Samuel Allis took his position at the school—Dr. Mather taught part time and practiced medicine part time. It is likely that Jonathan's sons studied under the tutelage of Dr. Mather and Samuel Allis in preparation for college, as it was the only school in Northampton. See: Betty Allen Chapter. *Early Northampton* (Northampton, MA: Daughters of the American Revolution, 1914), 56.
[31] Elisabeth D. Dodds, *Marriage to a Difficult Man,* 124.

descendants who claim him as their own. However, Jonathan would never have been able to have such an enduring influence for Christ had not his wife done all that was in her power to "render everything in the family agreeable and pleasant" for him, thereby freeing him to spend incalculable amounts of time in his study seeking the Lord.

Whether discussing physical descendants or spiritual ones, it is clear that the extent of Jonathan and Sarah's fruitfulness was because of their "uncommon union." Neither one of them would have been able to make such a lasting impact for Christ on their own. By God's grace, both Jonathan and Sarah will be able to claim untold spiritual and physical descendants for Christ at the last day. Glory to God for His incomprehensible grace!

Cross-bearing

It is impossible to write about a man and a woman who "counted all things as loss compared to the surpassing value of knowing Christ"[32] and who wanted to "know Him, and the power of His resurrection, and the *fellowship of His sufferings*, being conformed to His death,"[33] without chronicling the grace of God in the crosses He gave and enabled them to bear.

Life in the 1700's was particularly harsh for the American colonists. They were without medicine, modern conveniences, and rapid long-distance communication. They were surrounded by French and Indian wars, tension with Great Britain, life-threatening diseases, and rough winters. They were painfully aware of their dependence upon livestock and the fruit of the land, making some winters abundant and others meager. These were the normal conditions of every colonist in New England.

---

[32] Philippians 3:8
[33] Philippians 3:10

In addition, the Edwardses were given many unique crosses to bear as their portion "in filling up that which is lacking in Christ's afflictions."[34] For Sarah, one of them was the continual scrutiny she endured by the townspeople. Feeling the weight of interrogating eyes—whether at the marketplace, at church, or even at home—can cause the pressure to mount. Sarah was the envy of many townswomen—she was beautiful and intelligent. Moreover, she was blessed with a godly husband, eleven children,[35] and an unusually close relationship with the Lord. Couple these facts with the normal censorious spirit that many pastor's wives undergo, and Sarah became the subject of town gossip and slander. This is a difficult cup for a tender heart that seeks a blameless testimony for the Lord. It is also a bitter cup for someone prone to the sin of seeking men's approval. In fact, this is the reason why (coupled with her husband's disapproval of the way in which she handled a situation) Sarah began to sink into a depression. However, her cross proved to be the way to glory. It was through her inability to please men that she began to call out to the One who would "not

---

[34] Colossians 1:24. This verse does not suggest that there was anything insufficient or lacking in Christ's redeeming work on the cross. Rather, it is a reference to Christ's on-going ministry through His Spirit in the churches to take the gospel to every creature and present every man to God "complete in Christ" (Colossians 1:28). It is a ministry call for the Christian to do his part in identifying with Christ crucified by suffering for the sake of the gospel. The Moravian call to missions summarizes it well: "May the Lamb that was slain receive the reward of His sufferings." The Bible reveals that Christ purchased men with His blood from every tribe, tongue, people and nation (Revelation 5:9). It is the privilege of the Christian to take the gospel of Jesus Christ to every people, knowing that among them there are some for whom Christ died, and counting Him worthy of the necessary suffering to bring them the good news. This is what the Moravians meant by "May the Lamb receive the reward of His sufferings" and what the apostle Paul meant by "filling up that which is lacking in Christ's afflictions."

[35] At the time of her narrative, Sarah had only given birth to seven out of her eleven children.

30

bring a charge against [her]."[36] The Lord met her in the most unusual way, graced her with an entire resignation to Him, and brought to completion in her heart (and in the hearts of many others) what we know of today as the First Great Awakening. Sarah gave full testimony to this extraordinary work of grace in her narrative.

Dismissed

The second cross Jonathan and Sarah were given was Jonathan's dismissal from the church he loved and served for twenty-three years. When Jonathan accepted the pastorate at Northampton, the practice of the church (which was established by his distinguished grandfather, Solomon Stoddard) was to allow unregenerate members to partake of the Lord's Supper, believing that it was a "converting ordinance."[37] Initially, the practice continued under Jonathan's leadership. However, as he continued to pray and study the Scriptures, he became convinced that the Lord's Supper is not a converting ordinance. The congregation scoffed as Jonathan made his conclusions known. It would be unusual for a congregation to resist his position unless they were enjoying the public approval of taking the Lord's Supper without being willing to repent of their sins and identify with Christ crucified.

When Jonathan withheld the Lord's Supper from a man who would not make a profession of faith, the crisis came to a head. Jonathan could not maintain a clear conscience before the Lord and admit the unconverted to the Lord's Table. The Lord's Supper

---

[36] Romans 8:33. It was this entire passage, Romans 8:31-39, which the Lord used to grace Sarah with a full surrender to Him concerning her reputation among men.
[37] Jonathan's grandfather, Solomon Stoddard, believed that the unregenerate were more likely to become converted through the means of partaking the Lord's Supper. This is not a commonly held position.

is a holy ordinance, representing the blood and body of Christ, with warnings against those who take it lightly.[38]

The townspeople were outraged. Jonathan proposed to hold congregational meetings after Sunday morning worship to explain the reasons behind his conviction, but he was denied. Instead, the church granted him Thursday afternoons. The Thursday afternoon meetings were crowded, but with curious visitors, not church members. A council of congregants and ministers was convened to review the situation. The council consisted of men chosen in part by the congregation and in part by Jonathan. Nevertheless, the congregation limited Jonathan's selection to the one county where the majority of ministers were against him. The council met and called for Jonathan's dismissal. The church ratified their decision by a vote of 200 to 23. David Hall, a member of the council, made this observation of Jonathan when the final verdict was pronounced against him:

> The faithful witness received the shock unshaken. I never saw the least symptoms of displeasure in his countenance the whole week, but he appeared like a man of God whose happiness was out of the reach of his enemies and whose treasure was not only a future but a present good, overbalancing all imaginable ills of life, even to the astonishment of many who could not be at rest without his dismissal.[39]

There is no doubt that a public dismissal of this magnitude would be a disgrace to any family—any family but the Edwards family, that is. As noted before, one of Sarah's besetting sins was

---

[38] I Corinthians 11:27-32
[39] Ian Murray. *Jonathan Edwards: A New Biography*, (Carlisle, PA: Banner of Truth, 1987), 327.

her focus on her reputation. However, during the two-week awakening described in her narrative, Sarah was enabled, by the Spirit of God, to completely surrender her reputation to God. Now with her husband's dismissal, she was put to the test. By God's grace, she followed her husband in loving the church[40] and submitting to God without shame or regret. Sarah was a "completer to a contender for the faith" in the truest sense, for when she was called upon to deny herself for the sake of the gospel,[41] she did not "shrink back,"[42] but gave glory to God.

Death of Her Daughter

Above all, the heaviest cross Sarah and Jonathan bore for the sake of the gospel was the death of their seventeen-year-old daughter, Jerusha.

Jerusha was the second oldest daughter. She was graced with a tender heart for the Lord at an early age. She was very much the *spiritual* offspring of her parents. Her father said that she was "a very pleasant and useful member of this household and one that was esteemed as the Flower of the Family."[43] In her late teenage years, an extraordinary man came to the Edwards' home to spend time with Jonathan. His name was David Brainerd.

---

[40] Jonathan remained in Northampton for almost a year, waiting on the Lord to reveal to him where to go next. Within that time, the Northampton church was unable to find someone to fill the pastorate. They requested that Jonathan preach for them, but for significantly less than his former salary. Jonathan agreed, and preached with a spirit of love, grace, and humility, never once mentioning or alluding to the schism that was between them.

[41] According to Puritan theologian John Owen, the Lord's Supper is the *display* of the gospel. For a spiritually sweet, theologically deep discourse on the Lord's Supper, read *John Owen on the Lord's Supper* edited by Jon D. Payne and *Jonathan Edwards' Sermons on the Lord's Supper*.

[42] Hebrews 10:38

[43] *The Works of Jonathan Edwards*, Vol. 1: cxxxvii.

David was a missionary to the Native Americans. He forsook whatever worldly comforts an American colonist had at the time to live with them. David was graced with an unusual passion for God and found no price too high to pay for the advancement of the gospel among them. He faced great hardships—wars, cold, hunger, and loneliness—but he esteemed Christ to be worth it. During his first year of ministry, he established a school for the Native American children and began translating the Psalms into their language. Several years later, he settled in New Jersey. Within his first year there, the Lord raise up a congregation of 130 Native American converts. His ministry was fruitful, but his health was deteriorating. He received offers to return to civilization to take a pastorate—but he refused. He wrote in his journal:

> [I] could have no freedom in the thought of any other circumstances or business in life. *All my desire was the conversion of the heathen, and all my hope was in God.* God does not suffer me to please or comfort myself with hopes of seeing friends, returning to my dear acquaintance, and enjoying worldly comforts.[44]

David, who had signs of tuberculosis since college, continued to minister the gospel to the Native Americans until death was imminent. In his final days, he traveled to the home of Jonathan Edwards. Jonathan knew death was knocking at his door, but he took David in anyhow.[45] Moreover, he allowed his seventeen-year-old daughter, Jerusha, to nurse him. What would make a promising, intelligent, beautiful young woman risk her life to nurse

---

[44] Jonathan Edwards. *The Life and Diary of David Brainerd* (Grand Rapids, MI: Baker Books, 1989), 174.
[45] David was orphaned at age 14. Jonathan was like a spiritual father to him.

a man dying of tuberculosis? It could have been the deep respect she felt for the man who gave his life for the sake of the gospel. However, many young women might admire such a man from afar yet not be willing to embrace his sickness. What would persuade her to do such a thing? It seems as if David and Jerusha had an "uncommon union" much like the one between Jonathan and Sarah. During his final days, David and Jerusha traveled together to Boston, hoping a change of scenery might restore his health—but his condition only worsened. As death drew near, David called over each member of the Edwards family to give his final words. Jonathan recorded David's last words to Jerusha:

> As my daughter Jerusha, who chiefly attended him, came into the room, he looked on her very pleasantly and said, 'Dear Jerusha, are you willing to part with me? I am quite willing to part with you. I am willing to part with all my friends . . . though if I thought I should not see you and be happy with you in another world, I could not bear to part with you. But we shall spend a happy eternity together.'[46]

David died October 9, 1747. Only four months later, Jerusha died. She had contracted tuberculosis from David. Her father, Jonathan, recorded his final observations of David and Jerusha in his publication of David's journal entitled *The Life and Diary of David Brainerd.* Jonathan wrote:

> Since this, it has pleased a holy and sovereign God to take away this my dear child by death . . . in the eighteenth year of her age.[47] *She was a person of much the same spirit with Mr. Brainerd.* She

---

[46] Jonathan Edwards, *The Life and Diary of David Brainerd*, 375.

[47] Jerusha died two months short of her eighteenth birthday.

had constantly taken care of him and attended him in his sickness for nineteen weeks before his death, *devoting herself to it with great delight, because she looked on him as an eminent servant of Jesus Christ.*

In this time, he had many conversations with her on the things of religion; and in his dying sense, often expressed to us, her parents, his great satisfaction concerning her true piety and his confidence that he should meet her in heaven. [He also expressed] his high opinion of her, not only as a true Christian, but a very eminent saint; one whose world was uncommonly fed and entertained with things that appertain to the most spiritual, experimental, and distinguishing parts of religion. [He regarded her as] one who, by the temper of her mind, was fitted to deny herself for God and to do good beyond any young woman whatsoever he knew of. *She had manifested a heart uncommonly devoted to God* in the course of her life and many years before her death. [She] said on her deathbed that she had not seen one minute for several years wherein she desired to live one minute longer for the sake of any other good in life but doing good, living to God, and doing what might be for His glory.[48]

Jerusha was buried beside David. There is little doubt that David and Jerusha shared an "uncommon union." Their hearts were knit by spiritual ties that superseded all earthly barriers and circumstances. Their love was so pure and sweet that it was to be consummated in the full, unveiled presence of God in heaven.

What kind of love would cause a young woman to stay beside a man whose body was literally wasting away before her eyes; a

---

[48] Jonathan Edwards, *The Life and Diary of David Brainerd*, 375.

man who needed tending day *and* night with violent fevers, hot sweats, vomiting, spewing forth blood, and agonizing cries of pain; a man whose physical appearance was disfigured by disease? What kind of love would enable a young woman to knowingly risk her life for a man, who since the first day she met him, would never be able to love her in return, as far as the world knows it? What kind of love would move a young woman to enter into the death of a man who had no promise for her future, except death itself? It could be none other than that "uncommon union" of two spirits knit together in Christ, experiencing a depth of love and joy together in His Spirit that few understand or achieve.

It should not surprise us that the offspring of the "uncommon union" of Jonathan and Sarah enjoyed the blessing of a similar union. Yet, the union of David and Jerusha seemed to be even more exceptional. It surpassed that of her parents, in that it was *only* a spiritual union, and it united them in death. "Greater love has no one than this, that one lay down his [or her] life for his friends."[49] Truly, their union was an *unprecedented union*. While such a union is profoundly moving, it did not come without a price— not only for Jerusha but for her parents. Jonathan and Sarah knew full well the dangers of bringing tuberculosis into their home. Furthermore, they knew that in giving their beautiful, young daughter to David as his nurse, they were, in a sense, relinquishing her to the Lord. Jonathan wrote to a dear friend regarding Jerusha's death:

> Herein we have a great loss; but the remembrance of the remarkable appearances of piety in her from her childhood in life, and also at her death, are very comforting to us, and give

---

[49] John 15:13.

us great reason to mingle thanksgiving with our mourning. I desire your prayers, dear sir, that God would make up our great loss in Himself.[50]

The testimony of Jerusha's godliness provided comfort in their pain. According to Sarah's narrative, the lives of her children was something she had resigned to God years earlier.[51] The death of Jerusha proved the validity of her narrative. Although she loved her daughter deeply, and all the more because of their spiritual union in Christ, that same union was her source of comfort and reason to hope for a blessed reunion in heaven.

Sarah's favorite Bible passage, Romans 8:36-39, provides a fitting description of both David and Jerusha, and Jonathan and Sarah:

> Just as it is written, 'For Thy sake we are being put to death all day long; we were considered as sheep to be slaughtered.' But in all these things we overwhelmingly conquer through Him who loved us. For I am convinced that *neither death nor life*, nor angels nor principalities, nor things present nor things to come, nor powers nor height nor depth, nor any other created thing, shall be able to separate us from the love of God, which is in Christ Jesus our Lord.

---

[50] *The Works of Jonathan Edwards*, Vol. 1:cxxxvii.

[51] Sarah wrote in her narrative, "I found, so far as I could judge, an entire resignation to His will, and felt that if He should thus strip me of everything, that I would have an entire calm and rest in God, for it was His own, and not mine." It is also recorded of Sarah in *The Works of Jonathan Edwards* that, "She had long told her intimate friends that she had, after long struggles and exercises, obtained by God's grace, an habitual willingness to die herself or part with any of her most near relatives" (*Works,* Vol. 1: ccxxi).

Sarah found in Christ a love so large that it encompassed every human loss. She knew the death of her daughter was not in vain. It was for the sake of the gospel that Jerusha gave her life for one of Christ's most eminent servants. Even now in heaven, David and Jerusha, and Jonathan and Sarah, are experiencing joy inexplicable and full of glory before the throne, crying out, "Worthy is the Lamb!"

Missionary to the Native American Indians

Three years after the death of Jerusha, Jonathan was dismissed from the pastorate at Northampton. He remained in Northampton for a year, without position or salary, waiting on the Lord. When he heard that there was an opening at a mission post in Stockbridge to the Native Americans, the family packed their belongings and said "farewell" to Northampton. Life at Stockbridge was rugged. It was not for the civilized or faint of heart. Stockbridge was on the edge of the wilderness, and living conditions were harsh. The Edwardses were not only close to the French and Indian wars but literally in the middle of them. Jonathan preached two services—one for the few colonists and another for the Native Americans. He initially used a translator for his mission work until he could learn the language. While the people of Northampton regarded Jonathan's position at Stockbridge as a step down, in the eyes of God, it was a step up. Jonathan was moved from the middle of the ranks to the front line of the battle. He followed in the footsteps of David Brainerd by taking the gospel to those who had never heard.

It was also at Stockbridge that "Christ increased" and Jonathan "decreased."[52] Just as a grain of wheat must die and fall into the

---

[52] John 3:30

ground to bear fruit,[53] so Jonathan "died" and was "buried" in Stockbridge. Yet, while he was hidden there, he accomplished his greatest work of all—his written works. It was during this time that he was able to devote himself to the ministry of writing. Years later, his works sprang forth to bear fruit for the glory of God, all around the world, even to this day.

Truly, the cross[54] proved to be the way of glory for him. Sarah followed her husband into the wilderness. She quickly adjusted to pioneer life and made her home a beacon of light. She embraced the Native American people wholeheartedly. She was no longer in the limelight, yet she was no longer the talk of the town. She could say, like the apostle Paul, "I have learned to be content in whatever circumstances I am. I know how to get along with humble means, and I also know how to live in prosperity. I have learned the secret of being filled and going hungry, both of having abundance and suffering need. I can do all things through Christ who strengthens me." [55] Her mission work in Stockbridge gave even greater testimony to the work of God's grace as detailed in her narrative. Jonathan wrote to his father:

> My wife and children are well-pleased with our present situation. They like the place much better than they expected. Here, at present, we live in peace; which has of long time been an unusual thing with us. The Indians seem much pleased with my family, especially my wife.[56]

Jonathan established a school for the Native American children and taught them to read and write. He also taught them the

---

[53] Luke 12:24
[54] Of being dismissed from the church at Northampton
[55] Philippians 4:11-13
[56] *The Works of Jonathan Edwards,* Vol. 1: clxxxiii.

Scriptures and the Westminster Shorter Catechism. He witnessed a revival break out among them and by God's grace was able to establish a church. He was their advocate in every way. He loved them, and they loved him.

That We May Kiss the Rod

By this time, Jonathan and Sarah's third-born daughter, Esther, had married Aaron Burr, the president of the College of New Jersey.[57] They had two small children, Sarah, age four, and Aaron, age two. Aaron Sr. worked tirelessly to nurture the college in its infant stages and died suddenly at the age of forty-one from fever and exhaustion. Esther wrote her parents to request prayer, that she might not dishonor the Lord in her bereavement:

Dear Mother,

No doubt, dear Madam, it will be some comfort to you to hear that God has not utterly forsaken, although He has cast down. I would speak it to the glory of God's name that I think He has, in an uncommon degree, discovered[58] Himself to be an all-sufficient God, a full fountain of all good. Although all streams were cut off, yet the fountain is left full. I think I have been enabled to cast my care upon Him[59] and have found great peace and calmness in my mind, such as this world cannot give nor take. I have had uncommon freedom and nearness to the throne of grace. God has seemed sensibly near in such a supporting and comfortable manner that I think I have never experienced the like. God has helped me to review my past and present mercies with some heart-affecting degree of

---

[57] i.e., Princeton University
[58] revealed
[59] I Peter 5:7

thankfulness. I think God has given me such a sense of the vanity of the world, and uncertainty of all sublunary enjoyments, as I never had before. The world vanishes out at my sight! Heavenly and eternal things appear much more real and important than ever before. I feel myself to be under much greater obligations to be the Lord's than before this sore affliction. *The way of salvation by faith in Jesus Christ has appeared more clear and excellent;* and I have been constrained to venture my all upon Him, and have found great peace of soul in what I hope have been the actings of faith. Some parts of the Psalms have been very comforting and refreshing to my soul. I hope God has helped me to eye His hand in this awful dispensation, and to see the infinite right He has to His own and to dispose of them as He pleases.

Thus, dear Madam, I have given you some broken hints of the exercises and supports of my mind since the death of him whose memory and example will ever be precious to me as my own life. O, dear Madam! I doubt not but I have your and my honored father's prayers daily for me; but give me leave to entreat you both, to request earnestly of the Lord, that I may never despise His chastenings nor faint under His severe stroke; of which I am sensible there is great danger, if God should only deny me the supports that He has hitherto graciously granted.

O, I am afraid I shall conduct myself so as to bring dishonor on my God and the religion which I profess! No, rather let me die this moment than be left to bring dishonor on God's holy name. I am overcome—I must conclude, with once more begging, that as my dear parents remember themselves, they would not forget their greatly afflicted daughter (now a lonely widow) nor her fatherless children. My duty to my ever dear and honored parents, and love to my brothers and sisters. From, dear Madam, your dutiful and affectionate daughter, Esther.[60]

As one feels for Esther's plight, one cannot help to praise the God of her parents, who graced her to have such an overwhelming concern for His glory in the midst of her pain and who enabled her to cling to Christ and see Him more clearly in her greatest hour of need.[61]

Jonathan wrote Esther a letter of comfort. Regrettably, the letter is lost, but Esther's reply to his letter has been preserved. It reads:

To My Ever Honored Father.

Honored Sir, your most affectionate, comforting letter, by my brother Parsons, was exceeding refreshing to me; although I was somewhat damped by hearing that I should not see you until spring. But it is my comfort in this disappointment, as well as under all my affliction, that God knows what is best for me and for His own glory. Perhaps I counted too much on the company and conversation of such a near and dear affectionate father and guide. I cannot doubt but all is for the best; and I am satisfied that God should order the affair of your removal as shall be for His glory, whatever becomes of me.

---

60 *The Works of Jonathan Edwards,* vol. 1:ccxv

61 Esther wrote in a letter to a friend, "Had not God supported me by these two considerations; first, by showing the right He has to His own creatures, to dispose of them when and in what manner He pleases; and secondly, by enabling me to follow him [her husband] beyond the grave into the eternal world, and there to view him in unspeakable glory and happiness, freed from all sin and sorrow; I should, long before this have been sunk among the dead, and been covered with the clouds of the valley. God has wise ends in all that He doth. This thing did not come upon me by chance; and I rejoice that I am in the hands of such a God,' (*The Works of Jonathan Edwards,* Vol. 1:ccxv).

Since I wrote my mother a letter, God has carried me through new trials and given me new supports. My little son has been sick with a low fever ever since my brother left us and has been brought to the brink of the grave; but, I hope in mercy, God is bringing him back again. I was enabled after a severe struggle with nature to resign the child with the greatest freedom. God showed me that the children were not my own, but His, and that He had a right to recall what He had lent, whenever He thought fit; and that I had no reason to complain or say that God was hard with me. This silenced me. But O how good is God. He not only kept me from complaining but comforted me, by enabling me to offer up my child by faith, if ever I acted faith. I saw the fullness there was in Christ for little infants, and His willingness to accept of such as were offered to Him. "Suffer little children to come unto me, and forbid them not,"[62] were comforting words. God also showed me, in such a lively manner, the fullness there was in Himself of all spiritual blessings that I said, "Although all streams were cut off, yet so long as my God lives, I have enough." He enabled me to say, "Although Thou slay me, yet will I trust in Thee."[63] In this time of trial, I was led to enter into a renewed and explicit covenant with God in a more solemn manner than ever before; and with the greatest freedom and delight, after much self-examination and prayer, I did give myself and my children to God with my whole heart. Never, until then, had I an adequate sense of the privilege we are allowed in covenanting with God. This act of soul left my mind in a great calm and steady trust in God. A few days after this, one evening, in talking of the glorious state my dear departed husband must be

---

[62] Matthew 19:14
[63] Job 13:15

in, my soul was carried out in such large desires after that glorious state that I was forced to retire from the family to conceal my joy.

When alone I was so transported; my soul carried out in such eager desires after perfection and the full enjoyment of God to serve Him uninterruptedly, that I think my nature would not have borne much more. I think, dear Sir, I had that night a foretaste of heaven. This frame continued, in some good degree, the whole night. I slept but little, and when I did, my dreams were all of heavenly and divine things.[64] Frequently since, I have felt the same in kind, though not in degree. This was about the time that God called me to give up my child. Thus a kind and gracious God has been with me, in six troubles and in seven.[65]

But O, Sir, what cause of deep humiliation and abasement of soul have I on account of remaining corruption which I see working continually in me, especially pride. O, how many shapes does pride cloak itself in. Satan is also busy, shooting his darts. But blessed be God those temptations of his that used to overthrow me as yet have not touched me. I will just hint at one or two if I am not tedious as to length. When I was about to renew my covenant with God, the suggestion seemed to arise in my mind, "It is better that you should not renew it than break it when you have; what a dreadful thing it will be if you do not keep it!" My reply was, "I did not do it in my own strength." Then the suggestion would return, "How do you know that God will help you to keep it?" But it did not shake me in the least. Oh, to be delivered from the power of Satan as

---

[64] Esther's experience was much the same as Sarah's awakening, which is detailed in her narrative.
[65] Job 5:19

well as sin! I cannot help hoping the time is near. God is certainly fitting me for Himself; and when I think that it will be soon that I shall be called hence, the thought is transporting.

I am afraid I have tired out your patience and will beg leave only to add my need of the earnest prayers of my dear and honored parents, and all good people, that I may not, at last, be a castaway; but that God would constantly grant me new supplies of divine grace. I am tenderly concerned for my dear brother Timothy, but I hope his sickness will not be unto death but for the glory of God. Please give my duty to my honored mother and my love to all my brothers and sisters. I am, honored and dear Sir, with the greatest respect, your affectionate and dutiful daughter, Esther.[66]

Truly, she was a "daughter of Sarah."[67] The Lord graced her not only with the same godly character but even a similar spiritual awakening that resulted in a disposition of entire resignation and grace—she had the likeness of her mother in every respect.

After Aaron's death, his position at the college was vacant. The college called Jonathan to take his place. Jonathan was reluctant—he felt himself primarily a preacher, not an administrator. He prayed for months and eventually took the position. Once again, the family prepared to move. Jonathan needed to be in New Jersey immediately, so the family stayed behind to pack while Jonathan went ahead. He was to return for them in several months to help them move.

The presence of her father must have been a great consolation to Esther. What a comfort it must have been to have his strong

---

[66] *The Works of Jonathan Edwards,* vol. 1:ccxvii-ccxviii.
[67] A reference to Sarah, the wife of Abraham, from I Peter 3:6, as well as to Sarah Edwards

spiritual arm to rest upon. How delighted she must have been to introduce him to his grandchildren! Yet the joy would not last for long. After only three months, Jonathan died from a smallpox vaccine. Upon his deathbed, Jonathan spoke his last words to his daughters, Esther and Lucy,[68] which were to be given to his wife, Sarah:

It seems to me to be the will of God that I must shortly leave you; therefore, give my kindest love to my dear wife and tell her that the *uncommon union*, which has so long subsisted between us, has been of such a nature as I trust is spiritual, and therefore will continue forever; and I hope she will be supported under so great a trial and submit cheerfully to the will of God.[69]

After Sarah received the letter, she immediately replied to her daughters and wrote:

---

[68] Lucy went to New Jersey to assist her sister, Esther, with the children after Aaron's death. She stayed for an extended period of time and probably started her journey back to Stockbridge with Sarah and the two small children.

[69] *The Works of Jonathan Edwards* Vol. 1: clxxviii. The account of his death continued, "He said but very little in his sickness; but was an admirable instance of patience and resignation to the last. Just at the close of his life, as some persons who stood by, expecting he would breathe his last in a few minutes, were lamenting his death, not only as a great frown on the college, but as having a dark aspect on the interest of religion in general; to their surprise, not imagining that he heard or ever would speak another word, he said, 'Trust in God, and ye need not fear.' These were his last words. What could have been more suitable to the occasion? And what need of more? In these there is as much matter of instruction and support as if he had written a volume. This was the only consolation to his bereaved friends, deeply sensible as they were of the loss which they and the church of Christ had sustained in his death. God is all sufficient, and still has the care of His church. [It is said that] 'Edwards appeared to have the uninterrupted use of his reason to the last, and died with as much calmness and composure, to all appearance, as that with which one goes to sleep,'" (*Works*. Vol. 1: ccxx).

47

What shall I say? A holy and good God has covered us with a dark cloud. O that we may kiss the rod and lay our hands on our mouths! The Lord has done it. He has made me adore His goodness that we had him so long. But my God lives, and He has my heart. O what a legacy my husband, and your father, has left us! We are all given to God, and there I am, and love to be.[70]

How was Sarah able to respond with such grace during the temporary separation of her "uncommon union"? It is said:

She had long told her intimate friends that she had, after long struggles and exercises, obtained by God's grace a habitual willingness to die herself or part with any of her most near relatives. That she was willing to bring forth children for death and to resign him up whom she esteemed so great a blessing to her and her family, her nearest partner, to the stroke of death, whenever God should see fit to take him. And when she had the greatest trial, in the death of Mr. Edwards, she found the help and comfort of such a disposition. Her conduct on this occasion was such as to excite the admiration of her friends; it discovered that she was sensible of the great loss which she and her children had sustained in his death; and at the same time, showed that she was quiet and resigned and had those invisible supports which enabled her to trust in God with quietness, hope, and humble joy.[71]

Sarah wrestled with God and prevailed. He graced her to remain in a state of sweet submission and humble adoration even

---

[70] *The Works of Jonathan Edwards,* Vol.1: ccxxi.
[71] Ibid.

in the most painful of circumstances—the death of her deeply loved and venerated husband.

Sarah would have written more to Esther, but she was unable. Her daughter, Susanna, picked up where she left off, displaying that same pious spirit that is so characteristic of the Edwards family. She wrote:

My dear sister Esther, Mother wrote this with a great deal of pain in her neck which disabled her from writing anymore. She thought you would be glad of these few lines from her own hand. O sister, how many calls have we, one upon the back of another. O, I beg your prayers that we who are young in the family may be awakened and excited to call more earnestly on God that He would be our Father and Friend forever.

My father took leave of all his people and family as affectionately as if he knew he should not come again. On the Sabbath afternoon, he preached from these words, "*We have no continuing city, therefore, let us seek one to come.*" The chapter he read was Acts 20:1-38. O, how proper; what could he have done more? When he had got out of doors he turned about, "I commit you to God," said he. I doubt not but God will take a fatherly care of us if we do not forget Him.[72]

Sadly, Esther was never able to read the letters. Sixteen days after the death of her father, Esther died[73] and left behind two small orphaned children. Upon hearing the news, Sarah packed her bags and traveled by stagecoach to New Jersey, a trip that would take at least three weeks. Upon arriving, she received

---

[72] *The Works of Jonathan Edwards*, vol.1: ccxxi
[73] Most likely she died from the same small pox vaccine from which Jonathan died.

Esther's orphaned children to take back with her to Stockbridge. After a week of traveling, she stayed at an inn in Philadelphia. At the age of forty-nine, while grieving the sudden death of her husband and daughter, plus caring for two small children on a treacherous journey, she fell ill, having contracted a severe case of dysentery. Two witnesses noted that she did not speak much in her sickness as she was afflicted with "violent pain." They made this observation of her on her deathbed:

> She apprehended her death was near, then she expressed her entire resignation to go and her desire that He might be glorified in all things; and that she might be enabled to glorify Him to the last; and continued in such a temper, calm and resigned, till she died.[74]

From the moment of God's awakening grace upon her, as detailed in her narrative, until her death, she maintained a spirit of total submission and resignation to God, possessing no greater desire than that He be glorified in her body, "whether by life or by death."[75] Truly, her life and death testify to God's glorious grace and undying love.

---

[74] *The Works of Jonathan Edwards,* Vol. 1: ccxxii.
[75] Philippians 1:20

Introduction to Sarah's Narrative

Upon an initial reading of Sarah's narrative, the reader is captivated by the intimacy Sarah enjoyed in her relationship with Christ. At times, He was so near she could have touched Him. Her heart was lifted up, as it were, to heaven, so that she could "kiss"[76] Him. Her encounter reveals the depths of communion one can have with God and the freedom from sin and this world one can enjoy. It serves as a vision to pray for, a hope to attain, and a reality to surpass! It whets spiritual appetites, awakens holy desires, and rebukes dullness of spirit. O, that God might grace us with more of Himself and visit us, too!

What is the Narrative of Sarah Edwards?

Sarah's narrative is the written record of an unusual work of God's grace that occurred in a heightened sense over a two week period of time and continued to bear fruit until her death. God's work of grace was not limited to Sarah—He poured His Spirit upon many people in Northampton and all throughout the American colonies. However, according to her husband, the work of God's grace upon her was extraordinary, even in light of the Great Awakening. What exactly happened during those two weeks?

God Shed Abroad His Love into Her Heart

Sarah was blessed with an unusually clear sight of God and His love made manifest in Christ. She wrote, "God the Father, and the Lord Jesus Christ, seemed as distinct persons, both manifesting their inconceivable loveliness, mildness, and gentleness, and their

---

[76] Psalm 2:12

51

great immutable love to me." Again, she wrote, "My *mind* was so deeply impressed with the love of Christ and a sense of His immediate presence that I could with difficulty refrain from rising from my seat and leaping for joy." Sarah's experience of the love of God parallels the prayer that the apostle Paul prayed for the church at Ephesus:

> For this reason, I bow my knees before the Father . . . that He would grant you, according to the riches of His glory, to be strengthened with power through His Spirit in the inner man, so that Christ may dwell in your hearts through faith; and that you, being *rooted and grounded in love*, may be able to comprehend with all the saints what is the breadth and length and height and depth and to *know the love of Christ* which surpasses knowledge, that you may be *filled up to all the fullness of Him.* Now to Him who is able to do exceedingly, abundantly beyond all that we ask or think, according to the power that works within us, to Him be the glory in the church and in Christ Jesus to all generations forever and ever. Amen.[77]

The only way to be "filled up with God" (as Sarah experienced) is to be rooted and grounded in the knowledge of His love (which occurred as she meditated upon Romans 8:31-39). And the way to be rooted and grounded in His love is to make it one's *sole* ambition "to know . . . Christ and Him crucified." [78] Christ crucified is the pinnacle not only of all earth history but of all eternity. From all eternity past,[79] He was "the Lamb who *has been*

---

[77] Ephesians 3:14-20
[78] I Corinthians 2:2
[79] i.e., before He created the world

slain" from the foundation of the world.[80] For all eternity future,[81] He will be worshiped as "the Lamb who was slain."[82] In eternity present, He is worshiped as the Lamb who was slain.[83] All things in heaven and earth revolve around and point to the crucified, risen, and exalted Lamb. There is no knowledge, no experience, no revelation that is given, or that ever will be given, that is higher, deeper, or more glorious than Christ crucified. Christ's death, resurrection, and ascension is the culmination of all eternity. In fact, it will take all eternity to peel back layer after layer of the knowledge of the love of God in Christ, and still the saints will never get to the bottom of it! This is the occupation of the saints forever—to know the love of God in Christ and to worship Him because of it!

How does one know the love of God in Christ? It goes beyond hearing the tenets of the gospel. A person must have the eyes of his heart opened to behold the beauty of Christ crucified as revealed in the Scriptures. As the prophet Job said, "I have heard of Thee by the hearing of the ear, *but now my eye sees Thee.*"[84] Job did not mean that He saw the literal face of God, for "no man can see [God] and live."[85] He meant that He saw God in His beauty, worth, and holiness *by faith.* His breath was taken away by the sight of "the great, the mighty, and the awesome God,"[86] and his eyes were opened to his own guilt, sinfulness, and unworthiness in contrast. He repented in sackcloth and ashes.

---

[80] Revelation 13:8

[81] i.e., in heaven

[82] Revelation 5:9-14; 15:3; 22:1-5

[83] John 1:29; I Corinthians 15:1-8

[84] Job 42:5

[85] Exodus 33:20; See also John 1:18, "No man has seen God at any time."

[86] Deuteronomy 10:17

This is the sight of God that Sarah Edwards had in beholding Christ crucified.[87] At this sight the believer is "filled up to all the fullness of God."[88] O, that God might give us full sight of His Son! That He might "strengthen us in the inner man so that Christ might dwell in our hearts through faith."[89] That we might not be so near-sighted!

What happens to people when the Spirit of God opens the eyes of their hearts to behold the crucified and risen Christ in His splendor, beauty, and majesty? They instantly fall in love with Him.

They Fall in Love with Christ

When Christ crucified is unveiled before the eyes of the heart, the believer instantly falls in love with Him. To fall in love with Christ is to behold Him, and to be so overcome by His beauty, as to be consumed with adoration, awe, and love. It is to be "lovesick"[90] for Him—to desire Him completely and only, and to find all of one's pleasure in Him and Him alone. It declares, "I must seek Him whom my soul loves."[91] It is a holy inebriation.[92] It is to "drink deeply and imbibe"[93] of His love. It is an intimacy so rare that it fills one's entire being.[94] It shouts from the mountain tops, "I am my Beloved's and He is mine!"[95] It blissfully sings, "His mouth is full of sweetness, and He is wholly desirable. This is my

---

[87] Galatians 3:1. Paul wrote to the church at Galatia, ". . . before whose eyes Jesus Christ was publicly portrayed as crucified." The people of Galatia did not literally see Christ crucified, but they saw Him crucified with the eyes of their hearts, by faith.

[88] Ephesians 3:19

[89] Ephesians 3:16-17

[90] Song of Solomon 5:8

[91] Song of Solomon 3:2

[92] Song of Solomon 1:1; Ephesians 5:18

[93] Song of Solomon 5:1

[94] John 14:23; Ephesians 5:18

[95] Song of Solomon 6:3

Beloved and this is my Friend."[96] Secure in His love, it whispers, "I am my Beloved's and His desire is for me. Come, my Beloved, let us go out into the country. . . . There I will give You my love."[97]

Falling in love with Christ is similar to falling in love with a person, yet it is different in several respects. For one, to fall in love with Christ empowers a person to fulfill his biblical responsibilities rather than hindering him. It clears his mind rather than clouding it. It frees him from sin rather than entangling him. It spills over to bless every area of his life rather than concentrating on just one. It releases a person from self-centeredness rather than fueling it. It makes a person more reasonable, real, diligent, alive, loving, giving, and holy. It further conforms a person to the image of Christ, who lived every moment of His earthly life in perfect fellowship with the Father, in perfect submission to His will, in perfect likeness of His character, and in total dependence upon Him by His Spirit in all things.

Sarah Fell in Love with Christ

By God's grace, Sarah received a clearer sight of God than most. She was overcome with His love and the splendor of His beauty. In the words of Solomon, she was *lovesick*: "Sustain me with raisin cakes, refresh me with apples, because I am *lovesick*."[98] As she beheld Him by faith, she was melted into His image and transformed into His likeness. Her heart was lifted up to heaven to partake of the sweetest, most holy communion with God. She experienced a holy intercourse with God which she described as a constant flowing back and forth of love. Everything on earth seemed inconsequential, so long as she had Christ. The more she

---

[96] Song of Solomon 5:16
[97] Song of Solomon 7:10-12
[98] Song of Solomon 2:5

beheld Him in His holiness, the more she saw her own sinfulness and filth. She was grieved, humbled, and broken. Yet at the same time, she abounded in joy at the sight of Him, for the more she beheld His worth, in contrast to her own unworthiness, the more she could comprehend the breadth, length, height, and depth of His love in giving of Himself for her. O, the praise that involuntarily springs up at such sights! These sights were what God used to free her from sin, wean her from the world, and grace her to be surrendered to His providence. Moreover, they enabled her to overflow with love for the brethren, be full of concern for the lost, and be committed to His glory above all things.

Sarah Fainted with Love

Such sights of the incomprehensible love of God in Christ weakened Sarah physically and sometimes caused her to faint, as lovers occasionally do. However, Sarah's fainting was not from the passion of human love—it was from divine love. She was graced with glimpses of God's beauty that cannot be expressed in words. We do not know the *degree* of sight which God gave her, but we do know the *results*—they were entirely consistent with the Scriptures.

Her Experience of God's Love Was Based Solely on Scripture

Sarah remarked how the clouds of sin parted and her heart was transported as the Holy Spirit enlightened her mind with the truths of Romans 8:31-39. Her entire experience of God's love was based on Jesus Christ as He is revealed in the Scriptures; and she gave equal praise to the Father, Son, and Holy Spirit for their work of redemption. She was not subject to mysticism or emotional fancies, but her faith and love ascended to rare heights as she meditated upon Christ crucified.

The Results of Her Falling in Love with Christ

Freed From the Sin that Entangles

While Sarah was not completely free from all sin, she was delivered from a besetting sin that had been a stronghold in her life—the desire for the approval of men. In fact, her two-week narrative begins with her conviction, repentance, and deliverance from this long-seated sin. She detailed how she was brought to the point of total rest and resignation to God concerning it. Sarah was also delivered from her fear of other preachers being more mightily used of God than her husband and her envy of other congregants who received more grace than she.[99] She wrote, "[I realized that] I was to be entirely willing if it was God's pleasure . . . that other Christians should appear to excel me in Christian experience and in the benefit they should derive from ministers. . . . I was enabled, as I thought, to exercise full resignation and acquiescence in God's pleasure as to these things."

Weaned from the World

In conjunction with being delivered from her concern over the opinions and affairs of men, Sarah was freed from the allurement of the things of this world. She wrote, "The whole world, with all its enjoyments and all its troubles, seemed to be nothing. My God was my all, my only portion. . . . I seemed to be lifted above earth and hell, out of the reach of everything here below, so that I could look on all the rage and enmity of men or devils with a kind of holy indifference and an undisturbed tranquility." Again she

---

[99] It is worth noting that as Sarah was enabled to rejoice in the thought of others receiving more grace, God was pleased to lavish *her* with more grace.

wrote, "It appeared to me that the angels in heaven sung praises for such wonderful, free, and sovereign grace, and my heart was lifted up in adoration and praise. I continued to have clear views of the future world, of eternal happiness and misery, and my heart was full of love to the souls of men."

Humbled, Broken, and Grieved Over Her Sin

The more grace Sarah received, the more humbled and broken she became. Her single desire was to point all men away from herself to the only one who is worthy—Christ. She wrote, "I felt . . . a deep abasement of soul under a sense of my own unworthiness." Again, "The spiritual beauty of the Father and the Saviour seemed to engross my whole mind. It was the instinctive feeling of my heart that 'Thou art; and there is none beside Thee.' I never felt such an entire emptiness of self-love." Her humility was not only before God, but also in regard to men. She wrote, "I never before felt so far from a disposition to judge and censure others with respect to the state of their hearts, their sincerity, or their attainments in holiness as I did that morning."

Surrendered to God's Good Pleasure

Sarah's total surrender and resignation to God concerning the details of her life is one of the most "Christ-like"[100] qualities she exhibited. Sarah wrote, "I had an overwhelming sense of the glory of God as the Great Eternal All and of the happiness of having my own will entirely subdued to His will." Again she wrote, "Though it seemed to me infinitely better to die to be with Christ, yet I felt an entire willingness to continue in this world so long as God pleased, to do and suffer what He would have me. . . . I felt

---

[100] Matthew 26:39

an entire resignation to His will with respect to the kind and manner of death that I should die, whether on the rack, or at the stake, or any other tormenting death. I thought about how I had that day even been made very sensible and fully willing if it was God's pleasure and for His glory, to die in darkness and horror. . . . Yea, I am willing to live a thousand years a hell upon earth if it be most for the honor of God."

Overflowing in Love for God

The preeminent fruit of Sarah's two-week encounter with God was her awakening to the all-encompassing love of God in Christ and the subsequent eternal flame of love that burned in her heart for Him. Sarah wrote, "All night I continued in a constant, clear, and lively sense of the heavenly sweetness of Christ's excellent and transcendent love, of His nearness to me, and of my dearness to Him, with an inexpressibly sweet calmness of soul in an entire rest in Him. . . . There seemed to be a constant flowing and reflowing of heavenly and divine love from Christ's heart to mine." She continued, "My soul was so filled with love to Christ and love to His people that I fainted under the intenseness of the feeling." O, that God would grace us with such love!

Overflowing in Love for Others

As a result of being filled with the love of God in Christ, Sarah was overcome with concern for those who did not know Him. She wrote, "I felt a great earnestness of soul and engagedness in seeking God for the town that religion might now revive." Again, "At the same time, I felt compassion and love for all mankind."

Sarah also bore an undying love for the brethren, feeling intense love for the Spirit of Christ that dwelt within them, viewing every thought and act of charity toward them as love and devotion to Christ Himself. She wrote, "At night, my soul seemed to be filled with an inexpressibly sweet and pure love to God and to the children of God." She continued, "I was entirely swallowed up in God, as my only portion, and His honor and glory was the object of my supreme desire and delight. At the same time, I felt a far greater love for the children of God than ever before. I seemed to love them as my own soul. When I saw them, my heart went out towards them with an inexpressible endearedness and sweetness. I beheld them by faith in their risen and glorified state, with spiritual bodies refashioned after the image of Christ's glorious body, and arrayed in the beauty of heaven."

Eternally Minded

As Sarah beheld God in His splendor and majesty, she was graced with an unusual glimpse of eternity, both of the joy of glorified saints and the misery of unrepentant sinners. Her heart was moved with awe and adoration as well as inexpressible grief and concern. Such sights moved her to fuller consecration and dedication with regard to all social duties and missionary activity. She wrote, "I also realized, in an unusual and very lively manner, how great a part of Christianity lies in the performance of our social and relative duties to one another." Her husband testified to the change in her demeanor when carrying about her duties and responsibilities as well as her devotion to the furtherance of the gospel and the exaltation of His name.

A Holy Afterglow

After Sarah's encounter with God, she repeatedly said, "I experienced a delightful calm, peace, and rest in God." Her mind was clear and focused. She fulfilled her daily duties with greater fervor and devotion. She wrote, "I awoke in the morning . . . in the same happy frame of mind and engaged in the duties of my family with a sweet consciousness that God was present with me."

Committed to the Glory of God

The undeniable evidence of the validity of Sarah's narrative was her unshakable commitment to the glory of God—even to the point of horrific pain and suffering if God so willed it. One glance at His face and no price was too high, no suffering too steep, so long as He was glorified. She wrote, "The glory of God seemed to overcome me and swallow me up. Every conceivable suffering and everything that was terrible to my nature seemed to shrink to nothing before it." Again she wrote, "The glory of God seemed to be all, and in all, and to swallow up every wish and desire of my heart."

Jonathan and Sarah Both Testified to Her Encounter with God as a Work of Sanctification

Sarah detailed her encounter with God as a work of sanctification. She wrote, "I knew that the *foretaste of glory* which I then had in my soul came from Him and that I certainly should go to Him, as it were, to drop myself into the Divine Being and be swallowed up in God." She never defined her experience in terms of conversion. Rather, she described it as greater degrees of grace and foretastes of heavenly glory.

Likewise, her husband explicitly stated that this was not a work of conversion but sanctification. He wrote, "These things took place not in the giddy age of youth, nor in a new convert, or in an inexperienced Christian, but in one that was converted above twenty-seven years ago." Even before her two-week encounter she had a testimony of virtue and piety that surpassed that of most Christians.

Was Sarah Real?

Sarah was real. She struggled with depression. She struggled with jealousy. She struggled with the fear of men. She struggled with not wanting to live. She feared how she might die. God graced her with deliverance from these struggles, but as she continued to behold Him, she was made aware of the deeper corruption that still dwelt within. Sins that she never knew existed were discovered, confronted, wrestled with, and mortified. She continued in this manner until the day she was received in glory.

The validity of her narrative was tested by several trials: the death of Jerusha, the dismissal from Northampton, and the sudden death of her husband, Jonathan, and daughter, Esther. Certainly, there were other tests that she underwent which have not been recorded in history. There may have been failings. If there were, they did not have the upper hand, for she persevered in love and holiness, and continued to grow in grace, giving glory to God until her dying breath.

Section II

Sarah's Narrative

Part I

On Tuesday night, January 19, 1742, I felt very uneasy and unhappy at my being so low in grace. I thought I very much needed help from God. I found a spirit of earnestness to seek His help for more holiness. When I had been earnestly wrestling with God for quite some time, I felt within myself great quietness of spirit, unusual submission to God, and a willingness to wait upon Him with respect to the time and manner in which He should help me. Furthermore, I wished that He should take His own time and His own way to do it.

The next morning, I found a degree of uneasiness in my mind at Mr. Edwards' suggesting that he thought I had failed, in some measure, in point of prudence in a conversation that I had with Mr. Williams of Hadley the day before. I found that it seemed to bereave me of the quietness and calm of my mind to not have the good opinion of my husband. This I much disliked in myself, as arguing a want of a sufficient rest in God. I felt a disposition to fight against it, and to look to God for help, that I might have a full and entire rest in Him, independent of all other things. I continued in this frame from early in the morning until about ten o'clock, at which time the Rev. Mr. Reynolds came for morning prayer.

I had before this so entirely given myself up to God and resigned everything into His hands that I had for a long time felt myself quite alone in the world, so that the peace and calm of my mind, and my rest in God as my only and all-sufficient happiness, seemed sensibly above the reach of disturbance from anything but these two things: 1) my own good name and fair reputation among men—especially the esteem and just treatment of the people of this town; 2) and more especially, the esteem, love, and kind treatment of my husband. At times, indeed, I had seemed to be considerably elevated above the influence of even these things; yet, I had not found my calm, peace, and rest in God so sensibly, fully, and constantly above the reach of disturbance from them until now.

While Mr. Reynolds prayed, I felt an earnest desire that in calling on God he should say, "Father," or that he should address the Almighty under that appellation. On which the thought turned in my mind, "Why can I say, 'Father'? Can I now at this time, with the confidence of a child, and without the least misgiving of heart, call God my Father?" This brought to my mind two lines of Mr. Erskine's Sonnet:

I see Him lay His vengeance by,
And smile in Jesus' face.

I was thus deeply sensible that my sins did loudly call for vengeance, but then by faith I saw God "lay His vengeance by, and smile in Jesus' face." It appeared to be real and certain that He did so. I had not the least doubt that He then sweetly smiled upon me with the look of forgiveness and love, having laid aside all His displeasure towards me for Jesus' sake, which made me feel very weak and somewhat faint.

In consequence of this, I felt a strong desire to be alone with God, to go to Him, without having anyone to interrupt the silent and soft communion which I earnestly desired between God and my own soul. Accordingly, I withdrew to my chamber. I should have been mentioned that before I retired while Mr. Reynolds was praying, these words in Romans 8:34 came into my mind: "Who is he that condemneth? It is Christ that died, yea rather that is risen again, who is even at the right hand of God, who also maketh intercession for us." These words, along with the words which proceed them, "Who shall separate us from the love of Christ,"[101] occasioned great sweetness and delight in my soul. But when I was alone, the words came to my mind with far greater power and sweetness. Upon which I took the Bible and read the words to the end of the chapter. While I was reading, the words were impressed upon my heart with even greater power and sweetness. They appeared to me with undoubted certainty as the words of God, and as words which God did pronounce concerning me. I had no more doubt of it than I had of my being. I seemed, as it were, to hear the great God proclaiming thus to the world concerning me, "Who shall lay anything to thy charge?"[102] It had strongly impressed upon me how impossible it was for anything in heaven or earth, in this world or in the future, to ever separate me from the love of God which is in Christ Jesus. I cannot find language to express how *certain* this appeared—the everlasting mountains and hills were but shadows to it! My safety, happiness, and eternal enjoyment of God's immutable love seemed as durable and unchangeable as God Himself. Melted and overcome by the sweetness of this assurance, I fell into a great flow of tears and could not forbear weeping aloud. It appeared certain to me that God was my Father and Christ my Lord and Savior—that He was mine and I was His.[103] Under a delightful sense of the immediate presence and love of God, these words seemed to come over and over in my mind: "My God, my all; my God, my all." The presence

---

[101] Romans 8:35
[102] Romans 8:33
[103] Song of Solomon 2:16

of God was so near, and so real, that I seemed scarcely conscious of anything else. God the Father, and the Lord Jesus Christ seemed as distinct persons, both manifesting their inconceivable loveliness, mildness, and gentleness, and their great immutable love to me. I seemed to be taken under the care and charge of my God and Saviour in an inexpressibly endearing manner. Christ appeared to me as a mighty Saviour under the character of the Lion of the Tribe of Judah, taking my heart, with all its corruptions, under His care and putting it at His feet. In all things which concerned me, I felt safe under the protection of the Father and the Saviour, who appeared with supreme kindness to keep a record of everything that I did and of everything that was done to me, purely for my good.

The peace and happiness which I hereupon felt were altogether inexpressible. It seemed to be that which came from heaven—to be eternal and unchangeable. I seemed to be lifted above earth and hell, out of the reach of everything here below, so that I could look on all the rage and enmity of men or devils with a kind of holy indifference and an undisturbed tranquility. At the same time, I felt compassion and love for all mankind, and a deep abasement of soul under a sense of my own unworthiness. I thought of the ministers who were in the house and felt willing to undergo any labor and self-denial if they would but come to the help of the Lord. I also felt myself more perfectly weaned from all things here below than ever before. The whole world, with all its enjoyments and all its troubles, seemed to be nothing. My God was my all, my only portion. No possible suffering appeared to be worth regarding. All persecutions and torments were a mere nothing. I seemed "to dwell on high, and the place of defense to be the munitions of rocks."[104]

After some time, the two evils mentioned above, as those which I should have been least able to bear, came to my mind; namely, the ill treatment of the town and the ill will of my husband. But now, I was carried exceedingly above even these things, and I could feel that if I were exposed to them both, they would seem comparatively as nothing. At that time, there was a deep snow on the ground, and I could think of being driven from my home into the cold and snow, of being chased from the town with the utmost contempt and malice, and of being left to perish with the cold, as cast out by all the world, with perfect calmness and serenity. It appeared to me that it would not move me or in the least disturb the inexpressible happiness and peace of my soul. My mind seemed as much above all such things as the sun is above the earth.

Part II

I continued in a very sweet and lively sense of divine things, day and night, sleeping and waking, until Saturday, January 23. On that morning, I had a most solemn and deep impression on my mind that the eye of God was fixed upon me. I felt that He was observing what improvements I had made of those spiritual communications which I had received from Him, as well as the respect He caused to be shown to Mr. Edwards, who had then been sent to preach at Leicester. I was sensible that I was sinful enough to bestow it on my pride, or on my sloth, which seemed exceedingly dreadful to me. At night, my soul seemed to be filled with an inexpressibly sweet and pure love to God and to the children of God. I was given a refreshing consolation and solace

---

[104] Isaiah 33:16

of soul which made me willing to lie on the earth at the feet of the servants of God, to declare His gracious dealings with me, and to breathe forth before them my love, gratitude, and praise.

The next day, which was the Sabbath, I enjoyed a sweet, lively, and assured sense of God's infinite grace, favor, and love to me in taking me out of the depths of hell and exalting me to the heavenly glory and dignity of a royal priesthood.

On Monday night (Mr. Edwards being gone that day to Leicester) I heard that Mr. Buell was coming to our town. From what I had heard of him, and of his success, I had strong hopes that there would be great effects from his labors here. At the same time, I had a deep and affecting impression that the eye of God was ever upon my heart, and that it greatly concerned me to watch my heart to see to it that I was perfectly resigned to God with respect to the instruments He should make use of to revive religion in this town. Moreover, that I was to be entirely willing, if it was God's pleasure, that He should make use of Mr. Buell, and that other Christians should appear to excel me in Christian experience and in the benefit they should derive from ministers. I was conscious that it would be exceedingly provoking to God if I should not be thus resigned and earnestly endeavored to watch my heart, that no feelings of a contrary nature might arise. I was enabled, as I thought, to exercise full resignation and acquiescence in God's pleasure as to these things. I was sensible of the great reason I had to bless God for His use of Mr. Edwards hitherto. However, I thought if He never blessed his labors anymore, and should greatly bless the labors of other ministers, I could entirely acquiesce to His will. It appeared to me meet and proper that God should employ babes and sucklings[105] to advance His kingdom.

---

[105] Psalm 8:2

When I thought of these things, it was my instinctive feeling to say, "Amen, Lord Jesus! Amen, Lord Jesus!" This seemed to be the sweet and instinctive language of my soul.

On Tuesday, I remained in a sweet and lively exercise of this resignation. Love for and rest in God seemed to be in my heart from day to day, far above the reach of everything here below. On Tuesday night, especially the latter part of it, I felt a great earnestness of soul and engagedness in seeking God for the town, that religion might now revive, and that God would bless Mr. Buell to that end. God seemed to be very near to me while I was thus striving with Him for these things, and I had a strong hope that what I sought of Him would be granted. There seemed naturally and unavoidably to arise in my mind an assurance that now God would do great things for Northampton.

On Wednesday morning, I heard that Mr. Buell arrived the night before at Mr. Phelps' and that there seemed to be great tokens and effects of the presence of God there which greatly encouraged me. About an hour and a half after Mr. Buell came to our house, I continued in entire resignedness to God and willingness that He should bless his labors here as much as He pleased to the enlivening of every saint and to the conversion of every sinner in the town. These feelings continued afterward when I saw his great success. I never felt the least rising of heart to the contrary, but my submission was even and uniform, without interruption or disturbance. I rejoiced when I saw the honor which God put upon him, the respect paid him by the people, and the greater success attending his preaching than the preaching of Mr. Edwards. I found rest and rejoicing in it, and the sweet language of my soul continually was, "Amen, Lord Jesus! Amen, Lord Jesus!"

At three o'clock in the afternoon, a lecture was preached by Mr. Buell. In the latter part of the sermon, one or two appeared much moved, and after the blessing, when the people were going out, several others. To my mind there was the clearest evidence that God was present in the congregation on the work of redeeming love. In light of this, I was all at once filled with such intense admiration at the wonderful condescension and grace of God in returning again to Northampton that my soul was overwhelmed and my bodily strength taken away. This was accompanied with an earnest longing that those of us who were the children of God might now arise and strive. It appeared to me that the angels in heaven sung praises for such wonderful, free, and sovereign grace, and my heart was lifted up in adoration and praise. I continued to have clear views of the future world of eternal happiness and misery, and my heart was full of love to the souls of men. On seeing some that I found were in a natural condition, I felt a most tender compassion for them. While I remained in the meeting-house, I was especially, from time to time, overcome by the sight of those whom I regarded as the children of God, and who, I had heard, were lively and animated in religion. We remained in the meeting-house about three hours after the public exercises were over. During most of the time, my bodily strength was overcome. Joy and thankfulness filled my mind as I contemplated the great goodness of God. As I reflected upon this, I conversed with those who were near me in a very earnest manner.

When I came home, I found Mr. Buell, Mr. Christophers, Mr. Hopkins, Mrs. Eleanor Dwight, the wife of Mr. Joseph Allen, and Mr. Job Strong at the house. Seeing and conversing with them on the divine goodness renewed my former feelings and filled me with an intense desire that we might all arise and with an active, flowing, and fervent heart give glory to God. The intenseness of my feelings again took away my bodily strength. The words of one of Dr. Watts' Hosannas powerfully affected me; and in the course of the conversation, I uttered them as the real language of my heart, with great earnestness and emotion, "Hosanna to King David's Son, who reigns on a superior throne." While I was uttering the words, my mind was so deeply impressed with the love of Christ and a sense of His immediate presence that I could with difficulty refrain from leaping for joy. I continued to enjoy this intense, lively, and refreshing sense of divine things, accompanied with strong emotions, for nearly an hour. After which, I experienced a delightful calm, peace, and rest in God until I retired for the night. During the night, both waking and sleeping, I had joyful views of divine things and a complacential[106] rest of soul in God.

Part III

I awoke in the morning of Thursday, January 28th, in the same happy frame of mind and engaged in the duties of my family with a sweet consciousness that God was present with me. I was filled with earnest longings of soul for the continuance and increase of the blessed fruits of the Holy Spirit in the town. About nine o'clock, these desires became so exceedingly intense, especially as I saw numbers of people coming into the house who appeared to have a deep interest in religion. My bodily strength was much weakened at the sight, and it was with difficulty that I could pursue my ordinary avocations. About eleven o'clock, as I accidentally went into the room where Mr. Buell was conversing with some of the people, I heard him say, "O, that we, who are the children of

---

[106] Meaning "with pleasure, accommodating."

God, should be cold and lifeless in religion!" I felt such a sense of the deep ingratitude manifested by the children of God, being cold and dead in religion, that my strength was immediately taken away and I sunk down on the spot. Those who were near raised me and placed me in a chair. Then, from the fullness of my heart, I expressed to them in a very earnest manner the deep sense I had of the wonderful grace of Christ towards me, of the assurance I had of His having saved me from hell, of my happiness running parallel with eternity, of the duty of giving up all to God, and of the peace and joy inspired by an entire dependence on His mercy and grace. Mr. Buell then read a melting hymn of Dr. Watts concerning the loveliness of Christ, the enjoyments of heaven, and the Christian's earnest desire of heavenly things. The truth and reality of the things mentioned in the hymn made so strong an impression on my mind, and my soul was drawn so powerfully towards Christ and heaven, that I leaped unconsciously from my chair. I seemed to be drawn upwards, soul and body, from the earth towards heaven. It appeared to me that I must naturally and necessarily ascend thither. These feelings continued while the hymn was being read and during the prayer of Mr. Christophers. After the prayer, Mr. Buell read a hymn on the glories of heaven which moved me so exceedingly and drew me so strongly heavenward that it seemed as if my body was drawn upwards, and I felt as if I must necessarily ascend thither. At length, my strength failed me, and I sunk down. They laid me on the bed, where I rested for a considerable time, faint with joy. While lying down, I contemplated the glories of the heavenly world. After I had lain a while, I felt more perfectly subdued and weaned from the world and more fully resigned to God than I had ever been conscious of before. I felt an entire indifference to the opinions, representations, and conduct of mankind respecting me, along with a perfect willingness that God should employ some other instrument than Mr. Edwards in advancing the work of grace in Northampton. I was entirely swallowed up in God as my only portion, and His honor and glory was the object of my supreme desire and delight. At the same time, I felt a far greater love for the children of God than ever before. I seemed to love them as my own soul. When I saw them, my heart went out towards them with an inexpressible endearedness and sweetness. I beheld them by faith in their risen and glorified state, with spiritual bodies refashioned after the image of Christ's glorious body, and arrayed in the beauty of heaven. The time when they would be so appeared very near, and by faith, it seemed as if it were already present. This was accompanied with a ravishing sense of the unspeakable joys of the upper world. They were so plain and evident to the eye of faith that I seemed to regard them as begun. These anticipations were renewed over and over, while I lay on the bed, from twelve o'clock till four, being too much exhausted by emotions of joy to rise and sit up. During most of the time, my feelings prompted me to converse very earnestly with the pious women who were present on the spiritual and heavenly objects of which I had so deep an impression. A little while before I arose, Mr. Buell and the people went to meeting.

I continued in a sweet and lively sense of divine things until I retired to rest. That night, which was Thursday night, January 28th, was the sweetest night I ever had in my life. I had never before, for such a great length of time, enjoyed so much of the light, rest, and sweetness of heaven in my soul without the least agitation of body. The great part of the night I lay awake, sometimes asleep, and sometimes between sleeping and waking. But all night I continued in a constant, clear, and lively sense of the heavenly sweetness of Christ's excellent and transcendent love, of His nearness to me, and of my dearness to Him, with an inexpressibly sweet calmness of soul in an entire rest in Him. I seemed to perceive a glow of divine love come down from the heart of Christ in heaven, into my heart, in a constant stream of sweet light. At the same time, my heart and soul all flowed out in love to Christ, so that there seemed to be a constant flowing and reflowing of heavenly and divine love from Christ's heart to mine. I seemed to float or swim in these bright, sweet beams of the love of Christ, like the motes swimming in the beams of the sun or the streams of His light which come in at the window. My soul remained in a kind of heavenly elysium.[107] So far as I am capable of making a comparison, I think that what I felt each minute during the continuance of the whole time was worth more than all the outward comfort and pleasure which I had enjoyed in my whole life put together. It was a pure delight which fed and satisfied the soul. It was pleasure without the least sting or any interruption. It was a sweetness which my soul was lost in. It seemed to be all that my feeble frame could sustain of that fullness of joy which is felt by those who behold the face of Christ and share His love in the heavenly world. There was but little difference whether I was asleep or awake, so deep was the impression made on my soul. However, if there was any difference, the sweetness was the greatest and most uninterrupted while I was asleep.

As I awoke early the next morning, which was Friday, I was led to think of Mr. Williams of Hadley preaching that day in the town. I had to examine my heart to see whether I was willing that he, who was a neighboring minister, should be extraordinarily blessed and made a greater instrument of good in the town than Mr. Edwards. I was enabled to say, with respect to that matter, "Amen,

---

[107] Meaning "a state of eternal happiness"

Lord Jesus!" and to be entirely willing, if God pleased, that he should be the instrument of converting every soul in the town. My soul acquiesced fully in the will of God as to the instrument He chose to use, if only His work of renewing grace did but go on.

This lively sense of the beauty and excellency of divine things continued during the morning, accompanied with peculiar sweetness and delight. To my own imagination, my soul seemed to go out of my body to God and Christ in heaven. God and Christ were so present to me—so near me—that I seemed removed from myself. The spiritual beauty of the Father and the Saviour seemed to engross my whole mind. It was the instinctive feeling of my heart that "Thou art; and there is none beside Thee."[108] I never felt such an entire emptiness of self-love. By God's grace, I never had regard to any private, selfish interest of my own. It seemed to me that I was entirely done with myself. I felt that the opinions of the world concerning me were nothing and that I had no more to do with any outward interest of my own than with that of a person whom I never saw—Christ! The glory of God seemed to be all, and in all, and to swallow up every wish and desire of my heart.

Part IV

Mr. Sheldon came into the house about ten o'clock and said to me as he came in, "The Sun of Righteousness[109] arose on my soul this morning." Upon which I said to him in reply, "That Sun has set upon my soul all night! I have dwelt on high in the heavenly mansions. The light of divine love has surrounded me. My soul has been lost in God and has almost left the body." This conversation only served to give me a still livelier sense of the reality and excellence of divine things, and that to such a degree,

---

[108] II Samuel 7:22
[109] Malachi 4:2

as again to take away my strength and occasion great agitation of body. So strong were my feelings that I could not refrain from conversing with those around me in a very earnest manner on the infinite riches of divine love in the work of salvation. I continued in this frame until my strength entirely failed, my flesh grew very cold, and they carried me and set me by the fire. As I sat there, I had a most affecting sense of the mighty power of Christ which had been exerted in what He had done for my soul, and in sustaining and keeping down the native corruptions of my heart, along with the glorious and wonderful grace of God in causing the "ark"[110] to return to Northampton.

So intense were my feelings when speaking of these things that I could not forbear rising up and leaping with joy and exultation. I felt at the same time an exceedingly strong and tender affection for the children of God. I then realized, in a manner exceedingly sweet and ravishing, the meaning of Christ's prayer in John 17:21, "That they all may be one, as Thou Father art in Me, and I in Thee, that they also may be one in Us." This union appeared to me an inconceivable, excellent, and sweet oneness. At the same time, I felt that oneness in my soul with the children of God who were present. Mr. Christophers then read the hymn out of the Penitential Cries, beginning with, "My soul doth magnify the Lord, my spirit doth rejoice." The whole hymn was deeply affecting to my feelings; but when these words were read, "My sighs at length are turned to songs, the Comforter is come," I was so conscious of the joyful presence of the Holy Spirit that I could scarcely refrain from leaping with transports of joy. This happy frame of mind continued until two o'clock when Mr. Williams came in and we soon went to the meeting house. He preached on the subject

---

[110] The return of the "ark" is a reference to the Shekinah glory, or manifest presence of God, that dwelt above the ark of the covenant of Israel.

of the assurance of faith. The whole sermon was affecting me, but especially when he came to show the way in which assurance was obtained and its happy fruits. When I heard him say, "Those who have assurance have a foretaste of heavenly glory," I knew the truth of it from what I felt. I knew that I had tasted the clusters of the heavenly Canaan. My soul was filled and overwhelmed with light, love, and joy in the Holy Ghost, and seemed ready to go away from the body. I could scarcely refrain from expressing my joy aloud in the midst of the service. I had in the meantime an overwhelming sense of the glory of God as the Great Eternal All and of the happiness of having my own will entirely subdued to His will. I knew that the foretaste of glory which I then had in my soul came from Him and that I certainly should go to Him, as it were, to drop myself into the Divine Being and be swallowed up in God.

Part V

After the meeting was done, the congregation waited while Mr. Buell went home to prepare his lecture. It was almost dark before he came. In the meantime, I conversed in a very earnest and joyful manner with those who were with me in the pew. My mind dwelt on the thought that the Lord God Omnipotent reigns,[111] and it appeared to me that He was going to set up a Reign of Love on the earth and that heaven and earth were coming together. This so exceedingly moved me that I could not forbear expressing aloud my exultation of soul. This subsided into a heavenly calm, and a rest of soul in God, which was even sweeter than what preceded it. Afterward, Mr. Buell preached, and the same happy frame of mind continued during the evening, night, and next day. In the

---

[111] Revelation 19:6

forenoon, I was thinking of the manner in which the children of God had been treated in the world[112]—particularly of their being shut up in prison—and the folly of such attempts to make them miserable seemed to surprise me. It appeared astonishing that men should think by this means to injure those who had such a kingdom within them. Towards night, I was informed that Mrs. P had expressed her fears that I should die before Mr. Edwards' return, and that he should think the people had killed his wife. I told those present that I chose to die in the way that was most agreeable to God's will, and that I should be willing to die in darkness and horror if it was most for the glory of God.

In the evening, I read those chapters in John which contain Christ's dying discourse with His disciples and His prayer for them. After I had finished reading, while thinking on what I had read, my soul was so filled with love to Christ and love to His people that I fainted under the intenseness of the feeling. While reading, I felt a delightful acquiescence in the petition to the Father, "I pray not that Thou shouldst take them out of the world, but that Thou shouldst keep them from the evil."[113] Though it seemed to me infinitely better to die to be with Christ,[114] yet I felt an entire willingness to continue in this world so long as God pleased, to do and suffer what He would have me.

After retiring to rest and sleeping a little while, I awoke and had a very lively consciousness of God's being near me. I had an idea of a shining way, or path of light, between heaven and my soul, somewhat as on Thursday night, except that God seemed nearer to me, the way seemed more open, and the communication more immediate and free. I lay awake most of the night with a constant,

---

[112] i.e., persecuted
[113] John 17:15
[114] Philippians 1:23

delightful sense of God's great love and infinite condescension, and with a continual view of God as *near*, and as *my God*. My soul remained, as on Thursday night, in a kind of heavenly elysium.[115] Whether waking or sleeping, there was no interruption throughout the night to the views of my soul, to its heavenly light, and to His divine, inexpressible sweetness. I was without any agitation or motion of the body. I was led to reflect on God's mercy in giving me, for many years, a willingness to die. Not only that, but for the past two years, in giving me a willingness to live, that I might do and suffer whatever He called me to here. Before that, I often felt impatient at the thought of living. This then appeared to me, as it had often done before, to give me the greatest sense of thankfulness to God. I also reflected upon how God had graciously given me, for a great while, an entire resignation to His will with respect to the kind and manner of death that I should die, whether on the rack, or at the stake, or any other tormenting death. I thought about how I had that day even been made very sensible and fully willing, if it was God's pleasure and for His glory, to die in darkness and horror. But now, it occurred to me that when I had thus been made willing to live, and to be kept on in this dark abode, I used to think of living no longer than to the ordinary age of man. Upon this I was led to ask myself whether I was not willing to be kept out of heaven even longer than normal, and my whole heart seemed immediately to reply, "Yes, a thousand years if it be God's will and for His honor and glory." Then my heart, in the language of resignation, went further, and with great alacrity[116] and sweetness to answer, as it were over and over again, "Yes, and live a thousand years in horror if it be most

---

[115] Meaning "a state of eternal happiness"
[116] Meaning "cheerfulness, sprightliness; a cheerful readiness or promptitude to do some act; cheerful willingness."

for the glory of God. Yea, I am willing to live a thousand years a hell upon earth if it be most for the honor of God." But then I considered what this would be, to live a hell upon earth, for so long a time. I thought of the torment of my body being so great, awful, and overwhelming that none could bear to live in the country where the spectacle was seen. I thought of the torment and horror of my mind being vastly greater than the torment of my body. While thinking thus it seemed to me that I found a perfect willingness, sweet quietness, and alacrity of soul in consenting that it should be so if it were most for the glory of God. So there was no hesitation, doubt, or darkness in my mind attending the thoughts of it, but my resignation seemed to be clear, like a light that shone through my soul. I continued to say, "Amen, Lord Jesus! Amen, Lord Jesus! Glorify Thyself in me, in my body and my soul," with a calm and sweetness of soul which banished all reluctance. The glory of God seemed to overcome me and swallow me up. Every conceivable suffering, and everything that was terrible to my nature seemed to shrink to nothing before it. This resignation continued in its clearness and brightness the rest of the night, and all the next day, and the night following, to Monday in the forenoon, without interruption or abatement. All this while, whenever I thought of it, the language of my soul was with the greatest fullness and alacrity, "Amen, Lord Jesus! Amen, Lord Jesus!" On Monday afternoon, it was not quite so perceptible and lively, but my mind remained so much in a similar frame for more than a week that I could never think of it without an inexpressible sweetness in my soul.

Part VI

After I had felt this resignation on Saturday night, for some time as I lay in bed, I felt such a disposition to rejoice in God that I wished to have the world join me in praising Him. I was ready to wonder how the world of mankind could lie and sleep when there was such a God to praise! I could scarcely forbear calling out to those who were asleep in the house to arise, rejoice, and praise God! When I arose on the morning of the Sabbath, I felt a love to all mankind, wholly peculiar in its strength and sweetness, far beyond all that I had ever felt before. The power of that love seemed to be inexpressible. I thought, if I were surrounded by enemies who were venting their malice and cruelty upon me in tormenting me, it would still be impossible that I should cherish any feelings towards them but those of love, pity, and ardent desires for their happiness. At the same time, I thought if I were cast off by my nearest and dearest friends, and if the feelings and conduct of my husband were to be changed from tenderness and affection to extreme hatred and cruelty, and that every day I could so rest in God, that it would not touch my heart or diminish my happiness. I could still go on with alacrity[117] in the performance of every act of duty and my happiness remains undiminished and entire.

I never before felt so far from a disposition to judge and censure others with respect to the state of their hearts, their sincerity, or their attainments in holiness as I did that morning. To do this seemed abhorrent to every feeling of my heart. I also realized, in an unusual and very lively manner, how great a part of Christianity lies in the performance of our social and relative duties to one another. The same lively and joyful sense of spiritual and

---

[117] Ibid.

divine things continued throughout the day—a sweet love to God and all mankind and such an entire rest of soul in God that it seemed as if nothing could be said of me or done to me that could touch my heart or disturb my enjoyment. The road between heaven and my soul seemed open and wide all the day long. The consciousness I had of the reality and excellence of heavenly things was so clear, and the affections they excited so intensely that it overcame my strength and kept my body weak and faint the great part of the day. The night also was comforting and refreshing.

This delightful frame of mind was continued on Monday. About noon, one of the neighbors who was conversing with me said, "One smile from Christ is worth a thousand million pounds." The words affected me exceedingly and in a manner in which I cannot express. I had a strong sense of the infinite worth of Christ's approbation and love, and at the same time of the grossness of the comparison. It only astonished me that anyone could compare a smile of Christ to any earthly treasure. Towards night I had a deep sense of the awful greatness of God and felt with what humility and reverence we ought to behave ourselves before him. Just then Mr. W came in and spoke with a somewhat light, smiling air of the flourishing state of religion in the town which I could scarcely bear to see. It seemed to me that we ought greatly to revere the presence of God, and to behave ourselves with the utmost solemnity and humility when so great and holy a God was so remarkably present, and to rejoice before Him with trembling.[118] In the evening these words in the Penitential Cries, "The Comforter is Come!" were accompanied to my soul with such conscious certainty, and such intense joy, that immediately it

---

[118] Psalm 2:11

took away my strength, and I was falling to the floor. Some of those who were near me caught me and held me up. And when I repeated the words to the by-standers, the strength of my feelings was increased. The name "The Comforter" seemed to denote that the Holy Spirit was the only and infinite Fountain of comfort and joy, and this seemed real and certain to my mind. These words "The Comforter" seemed as it were immensely great enough to fill heaven and earth.

On Tuesday after dinner, Mr. Buell sat at the table and began to give a discourse on the glories of the upper world. This greatly affected me so as to take away my strength. The views and feelings of the preceding evening respecting the Great Comforter were renewed in the most lively and joyful manner, so that my limbs grew cold. I continued to a considerable degree overcome for about an hour, earnestly expressing to those around me my deep and joyful sense of the presence and divine excellence of the Comforter and of the glories of heaven.

It was either on Tuesday or Wednesday that Mr. W came to the house and informed what account Mr. Lyman, who had just come from Leicester, gave of Mr. Edwards' success in making peace and promoting religion at Leicester. The intelligence[119] inspired me with such an admiring sense of the great goodness of God in using Mr. Edwards as the instrument of doing good and of promoting the work of salvation that it immediately overcame me and took away my strength. On Wednesday night, Mr. Clark came in with Mr. Buell and some others to ask me how I felt. I told him that I did not feel at all times alike, but this I thought I could say, that I had given up all to God and that there is nothing like it—nothing like giving up all to Him, esteeming all to be His,

---

[119] i.e., information

83

and resigning all at His call. I told him that many a time within a twelve-month I had asked myself when I lay down how should I feel if our house and all our property in it should be burnt up, and we should that night be turned out naked. I wondered whether I could cheerfully resign all to God and whether I really believed that all belonged to Him so that I could fully consent to His will in being deprived of it. I found, so far as I could judge, an entire resignation to His will, and felt that if He should thus strip me of everything, that I would have an entire calm and rest in God, for it was His own and not mine. After this, Mr. Phelps gave us an account of his own feelings during a journey from which he had just returned. Then Mr. Pomeroy broke forth in the language of joy, thankfulness, and praise, and continued speaking to us nearly an hour, leading us all the time to rejoice in the visible presence of God and to adore His infinite goodness and condescension. He concluded by saying, "I would say more if I could, but words were not made to express these things." This reminded me of the words of Mrs. Rowe:

> More I would speak, but all my words are faint,
> Celestial Love, what eloquence can paint?
> No more, by mortal words, can be expressed;
> But vast Eternity shall tell the rest.

My former impressions of heavenly and divine things were renewed with so much power, life, and joy that my strength failed me, and I remained for some time faint and exhausted. After the people had retired, I had an even more lively and joyful sense of the goodness and all-sufficiency of God, of the pleasure of loving Him, and of being alive and active in His service. In reflecting upon it, I could not sit still but walked the room for some time in a kind of transport. The contemplation was so refreshing and delightful, so much like a heavenly feast within the soul, that I felt an absolute indifference as to any external circumstances. According to my best remembrance, this enlivening of my spirit continued so that I slept but little that night.

On the next day, Thursday, between ten and eleven o'clock, there was a room full of people gathering together. I heard two persons give a minute account of the enlivening and joyful influences of the Holy Spirit on their own hearts. It was sweet to me to see others before me in their divine attainments and to follow after them to heaven. I thought I should rejoice to follow the African servants in the town to heaven. While I was listening to the testimonies of the blessed appearances of God's presence with us, it affected me so powerfully that the joy and transport of the preceding night were again renewed. After this, they sang a hymn which greatly moved me, especially the latter part of it, which speaks of the ungratefulness of not having the praises of Christ always on our tongues. Those last words of the hymn seemed to fasten on my mind. As I repeated them over, I felt such intense love to Christ and so much delight in praising Him that I could hardly forbear leaping from my chair and singing aloud for joy and exultation. I continued thus extraordinarily moved until about one o'clock when the people went away.

Sereno's Commentary on Sarah's Narrative

I am well aware that very different views will be formed of the preceding narrative by different individuals. Those who have no conception of what is meant by the religion of the heart will doubtless pronounce it the offspring of a diseased body or a distempered brain. Others, who profess the religion of Christ but whose minds only come in contact with things that are merely *palpable*—with nothing but what they can either see, or hear, or feel, or taste—will probably regard it as the effect of mere enthusiasm. While others, who are both more intellectual and more spiritual in their objects of contemplation, will at once perceive that the state of mind therein described is one to which they themselves are chiefly or wholly strangers. They will, therefore, very naturally and rationally, wish to learn of the individual who was the subject of these spiritual discoveries as well as of their actual effect upon her character. On these points, the testimony of Mr. Edwards is full and explicit, and from his authority, we state the following facts.

Jonathan's Edition of Sarah's Narrative

I have been particularly acquainted with many persons who have been the subjects of the high and extraordinary transports of the present day. But the highest transports I have been acquainted with, where the affections of admiration, love, and joy in God have been raised to the highest pitch, are those of Mrs. Sarah Edwards. In view of the glory of the divine perfections of Christ and His excellencies, her soul has been, as it were, perfectly overwhelmed and swallowed up with light and love, with a sweet solace and rest, and with a joy of soul altogether unspeakable. She has more than once continued for five or six hours together, without interruption, in a clear and lively view of the infinite beauty and amiableness of Christ's person and the heavenly sweetness of His transcendent love. So that (to use her own expressions) her soul remained in a kind of heavenly elysium.[120] Her soul seemed to swim, as it were, in the rays of Christ's love, like a little mote swimming in the beams of the sun that come in through the window. Her heart was swallowed up in a kind of glow of Christ's love coming down as a constant stream of sweet light. At the same time, her soul seemed to be flowing out back in love to Him, so that there was a constant flowing and reflowing from heart to heart. Her soul dwelt on high, was lost in God, and seemed almost to leave the body. Her mind dwelt in a pure delight that fed and satisfied it, enjoying pleasure without the least sting or any interruption. And what was enjoyed in a single minute of the whole space, which was many hours, was worth more than all the outward comfort and pleasure of the whole life put together. This

---

[120] State of eternal happiness

was without being in any trance or at all deprived of the exercise of any of the bodily senses or mental faculties. This heavenly delight has been enjoyed for years together, though not as frequently, nor for such long periods at a time, nor to such heights, as recently. Extraordinary views of divine things and the religious affections were frequently attended with very great effects on her body. Nature often sunk under the weight of divine discoveries, and the strength of her body was taken away. She was so consumed with the love of God in Christ that she was deprived of all ability to stand or speak. Sometimes her hands were clenched and her flesh grew cold from a weakness produced by an overwhelming sense of God's love, but her senses remained. She had utterly fallen in love with God, and her soul was so overcome with admiration, and a kind of omnipotent joy, so as to cause her to unavoidably leap with all her might in great joy and exultation. At the same time, she was so strongly drawn towards God and Christ in heaven that it seemed to her that her soul and body would, as it were of necessity, mount up, leave the earth, and ascend thither.

Her passionate love for Christ, and the effects it had on her body, was not owing to the influence of example but began about seven years ago, when there was no such enthusiastical season such as there is now. It was a very dead time through the land. Her strong affections toward God arose from no distemper caught from Mr. Whitefield or Mr. Tennant because they began before either of them came into the country. Near three years ago, they greatly increased upon an extraordinary self-dedication, renunciation of the world, and resignation of all to God, which were all made in view of God's excellency, in high exercise of love to Him, and in rest and joy in Him. Since that time, they have been very frequent and in higher degree, upon another new resignation of all to God, with a yet greater fervency and delight of soul. Her body often fainted in light of the overwhelming sense of the love of Christ. These effects appeared in a higher degree still last winter, when upon acceptance of God as the only portion and happiness of the soul, she resigned the whole world with the dearest enjoyments in it and renounced it all as dirt and dung. All that is pleasant and glorious, and all that is terrible in this world, seemed perfectly to vanish into nothing. Nothing was left but God, in whom the soul was perfectly swallowed up in an infinite ocean of blessedness. Since this time, there have often been great agitations of body and unavoidable leaping for joy. Her soul dwelt, almost without interruption, in a kind of paradise. Very often she was in high transports, disposed to speak to others concerning the great and glorious things of God in Christ and the eternal world in a most earnest manner and with a loud voice. These effects on her body did not arise from any bodily distemper or weakness because she had been in a good state of health.

This great rejoicing has been with trembling, with a deep and lively sense of the greatness and majesty of God, and with a view of her own exceeding littleness and vileness. Spiritual joys in her were never attended with the least appearance of laughter or lightness but with a peculiar abhorrence of such irreverence. These high transports, when past, have had abiding effects. There was an increase of sweetness, rest, and humility upon her soul, along with a new engagedness of heart to live to God's honor and to watch and fight against sin. Furthermore, these things took place not in the giddy age of youth, nor in a new convert, or in an inexperienced Christian, but in one that was converted above twenty-seven years ago. She was neither converted nor educated in that enthusiastic town of Northampton (as some may be ready to call it) but in a town and family which none suspected of enthusiasm. These effects found in her have been, in an uncommon manner, growing and rising by very sensible degrees to higher love to God, weanedness from the world, mastery over sin and temptation, through great trials and conflicts, long-continued struggling and fighting with sin, earnest and constant prayer, labor in religion, and engagedness of mind in the use of all means of grace, attended with a great exactness of life. This growth has been attended not only with a great increase of religious affections but with a wonderful alteration of her outward behavior, which has been visible to those who are most intimately acquainted with her so that she has appeared to have become, as it were, a new person. She has lived so much more above the world, and in a greater degree of steadfastness and strength in the way of duty and self-denial, maintaining the Christian conflict against temptations, and conquering from time to time under great trials. She has persisted in an unmoved, untouched calm and rest under the changes and accidents of time. She had formerly, in lower degrees of grace, been subject to unsteadiness and many ups and downs in the frame of her mind. She was under great disadvantages through a vaporous [121] habit of body, and often subject to and at times almost overcome with melancholy, beginning as early as in her youth. However, the strength of grace and divine light has of late wholly conquered these disadvantages and carried her mind, in a constant manner, quite above all such effects. Since that resignation spoken of before, made near three years ago, everything of that nature seems to be overcome and

---

[121] Webster's 1828 Dictionary defines vapors as splenetic (melancholy, anger, or vexation). Most likely, Sarah had previously suffered physical symptoms from stress. However, since God's "awakening" grace upon her, though her body still responded to stress, her heart and soul were above the stress her body felt. Rather than being agitated or depressed during times of stress, as before, she had a sweet calm and resignation even in the midst of trials and pain. This was a testimony to God's grace!

crushed by the power of faith and trust in God and resignation to Him. She has remained in an uninterrupted rest, humble joy in God, and assurance of His favor without one hour's melancholy or darkness from that day to this. Vapors[122] have had great effects on her body, such as they used to have before, but the soul has been always out of their reach. And this steadfastness and constancy have remained through great outward changes and trials, such as times of the most extreme pain and the apparent hazard of immediate death.

These transporting views and rapturous affections are not attended with any enthusiastic disposition to follow impulses or any supposed prophetical revelations. Nor have they been observed to be attended with any appearance of spiritual pride. Rather, they have been with great increase of humility and meekness and a disposition in honor to prefer others.[123] It is worth mentioning that when these discoveries and holy affections were evidently at the greatest height—which began early in the morning of the holy Sabbath and lasted for days together, melting her down in the deepest humility and poverty of spirit, reverence and resignation, sweet meekness and universal benevolence—two things were felt in a remarkable manner.

First, she had a peculiar aversion to judging other professing Christians of good standing in the visible church with respect to their conversion or degrees of grace. She also had an aversion to intermeddling with that matter, so much as to determine against and condemn others in the thoughts of the heart. Such things appeared hateful, as not agreeing with that lamb-like humility, meekness, gentleness, and charity which the soul then, above other times, saw to be beautiful. The disposition she felt was to prefer

---

[122] Ibid.
[123] Romans 12:10

93

others to self and to hope that they saw more of God and loved Him better. However, before this time, under smaller discoveries and feebler exercises of divine affection, she had a disposition to censure and condemn others.

Secondly, another thing that was felt at that time was a very great sense of the importance of moral social duties and how great a part of religion lay in them. There was such a new sense and conviction of this beyond what had been before, that it seemed to be as it were a clear discovery then made to the soul. In general, there has been a very great increase of a sense of these two things as divine views and divine love have increased.

The things already mentioned have been attended also with an extraordinary sense of the awful majesty, greatness, and holiness of God, so as sometimes to overwhelm soul and body. She also had a sense of the piercing, all-seeing eye of God, so as to take away bodily strength, along with an extraordinary view of the infinite terribleness of the wrath of God and the ineffable misery of sinners who are exposed to this wrath. Sometimes the exceeding pollution of her own heart as a sink of all manner of abomination, and the dreadfulness of an eternal hell of God's wrath, opened to view both together. There was a clear view of a desert of that misery, and that by the pollution of the best duties, by the irreverence and want of humility that attended once speaking of the holy name of God when done in the best manner that ever it was done. The strength of the body was very often taken away with a deep mourning for sin as committed against so holy and good a God. Sometimes it was by an affecting sense of actual sin, sometimes by indwelling sin in particular, and sometimes by the consideration of the sin of the heart as appearing in a particular thing. For instance, she grieved that there was no greater forwardness and readiness to self-denial for God and

Christ who had so denied Himself for us. Yea, sometimes the consideration of sin in only speaking one word concerning the infinitely great and holy God has been so affecting as to overcome the strength of nature.[124] She had a very great sense of the certain truth of the great things revealed in the gospel. Furthermore, she had an overwhelming sense of the glory of the work of redemption, of the way of salvation by Jesus Christ, and of the glorious harmony of the divine attributes appearing therein, such as how mercy and truth are met together, and righteousness and peace have kissed each other.[125] A sight of the fullness and glorious sufficiency of Christ has been so affecting as to overcome her body. She possessed a constant, immovable trust in God through Christ, with a great sense of His strength and faithfulness, the sureness of His covenant, and the immutability of His promises, which made the everlasting mountains and perpetual hills[126] appear as mere shadows in comparison.

Sometimes the sufficiency and faithfulness of God as the covenant God of His people appeared in these words, "I AM THAT I AM,"[127] in so affecting a manner as to overcome the body. A sense of the glorious, unsearchable, unerring wisdom of God in His works, both of creation and providence, was such as to swallow up the soul and overcome the strength of the body. There was a sweet rejoicing of her soul at the thoughts of God being infinitely and unchangeably happy, and an exulting gladness of heart that God is self-sufficient, infinitely above all dependence, reigns over all, and does His will with absolute and uncontrollable power and sovereignty. A sense of the glory of the Holy Spirit, as

---

[124] Possibly meaning in contrast to the many praises that He deserves
[125] Psalm 85:10
[126] Habakkuk 3:6
[127] Exodus 3:14

the great Comforter,[128] was such as to overwhelm both soul and body. Only the mere mentioning of the word "Comforter" would immediately take away all strength. That word, "Comforter," seemed great enough to fill heaven and earth. She had a most vehement and passionate desire of the honor and glory of God's name. She maintained a sensible, clear, and constant preference of it, not only to her own temporal interest but to her spiritual comfort in this world. She possessed a willingness to suffer the hidings of God's face and to live and die in darkness and horror if God's honor should require it—and to have no other reward for it but that God's name should be glorified, although so much of the sweetness of the light of God's countenance had been experienced. A great lamenting of ingratitude and the defect of love to God took away her bodily strength. *She very often felt vehement longings and faintings after more love to Christ* and greater conformity to Him. She especially longed after these two things—to be more perfect in humility and adoration. The flesh and heart seemed often to cry out for lying low before God and to fall down before His throne. She felt a great delight in singing praises to God and Jesus Christ, longing that this present life may be, as it were, one continued song of praise to God. She had a longing to sing this life away and an overcoming pleasure in the thoughts of spending an eternity in song and praise to God. Together with living by faith to a great degree, she had a constant and extraordinary distrust of her own strength and wisdom, as well as a great dependence on God for His help, in order to be able to perform anything to God's acceptance and to be restrained from the most horrid sins.

A sense of the black ingratitude of true saints as to their coldness and deadness in religion and to their setting their hearts

---

128 John 14:26

on the things of this world overcame the bodily frame. She had great longings that all the children of God might be lively in religion, fervent in love, and active in the service of God. Moreover, when she saw appearances of this in others, she rejoiced in beholding the pleasant sight, which produced a joy of soul having been too great for the body. She took pleasure in the thoughts of watching and striving against sin, fighting through the way to heaven, filling up this life with hard labor, and bearing the cross of Christ as an opportunity to give God honor. She did not desire to rest from labors for Christ till she arrived in heaven and abhorred the thoughts of it, and seemed astonished that God's own children should be backward to strive and deny themselves for God. There were earnest longings that all God's people might be clothed with humility and meekness, like the Lamb of God, and feel nothing in their hearts but love and compassion for all mankind. She possessed great grief when anything to the contrary appeared in any of the children of God such as bitterness, fierceness of zeal, censoriousness, reflecting uncharitably on others, and disputing with any appearance of heat of spirit. She maintained a deep concern for the good of others' souls. She had a melting compassion to those that looked on themselves as in a state of nature, and to saints under darkness, so as to cause her body to faint. She had a universal benevolence to mankind with a longing to embrace the whole world in the arms of pity and love. When she thought about suffering from enemies who were possessed with the utmost conceivable rage and cruelty, she maintained a disposition of fervent love and pity to them, as far as could be realized in thought. Sometimes a disposition was felt to a life given up to mourning alone in a wilderness over a lost and miserable world. She felt such compassion for men in the bondage of rage and cruelty that she could not rest but had to go to God in prayer and pour out her soul for them. She felt earnest desires that the work of God, now in the land, may be carried on with greater purity and freedom from all bitter zeal, censoriousness, spiritual pride, and hot disputes. She possessed a vehement and constant desire for the setting up of Christ's kingdom on the earth as a kingdom of holiness, purity, love, peace, and happiness to mankind.

Her soul often entertained, with unspeakable delight, the thoughts of heaven as a world of love, where love shall be the saints' eternal food. She saw it as a place where the saints shall dwell in light, swim in an ocean of love, and where the very air and breath will be nothing but love. She felt love to the people of God for bearing the image of Christ and as those who will in a very little time shine in His perfect image. Her strength was very often taken away with longings that others might love God more, serve Him better, and have more of His comfortable presence than even she herself had. She desired to follow the whole world to heaven, or that everyone should go before, and be higher in grace and happiness, not by her diminution, but by others' increase. This experience included a delight in conversing on religious subjects and in seeing Christians talking of the most spiritual and heavenly things in religion in a lively and feeling manner. Very frequently she was overcome with the pleasure of such conversation. She felt a great sense of the importance of the duty of charity to the poor and how much the generality of Christians come short in the practice of it. There was also a great sense of the need that ministers have more of the Spirit of God, at this day especially. She labored in most earnest longings and wrestlings with God for other ministers so as to take away her bodily strength. She also maintained the greatest, fullest, longest, and most constant assurance of the favor of God and of a title to future glory that ever I saw any appearance of in any person. She especially enjoyed as of late (to use her own expression) "the riches of full assurance."[129] Formerly, she had a longing to die with something of impatience; but lately, since that resignation fore-mentioned about three years ago, she maintained an uninterrupted entire resignation to God with respect to life or death, sickness or health, ease or pain, which has remained unchanged and unshaken, even under extreme and violent pains, and in times of threatenings of immediate death. But notwithstanding this patience and submission, the thoughts of death and the Day of Judgment have always been exceeding sweet to her soul. This resignation is also attended with a constant resignation of the lives of dearest earthly friends, even when some of their lives have been imminently threatened. She often expressed the sweetness of the liberty of having wholly left the world, and of having renounced all for God, and of having nothing but God, in whom is an infinite fullness. These things have been attended with a constant sweet peace, calm, and serenity of soul without any cloud to interrupt it. She had a continual rejoicing in all the works of God's hands, the works of nature, and God's daily works of providence, all appearing with a sweet smile upon them. She maintained a wonderful access to God by prayer, as it were, seeing Him by faith and immediately conversing with Him, as if Christ were here on earth, sitting on a visible throne, to be approached and conversed with.

She has had frequent, plain, sensible, and immediate answers to prayer, all tears wiped away, all former troubles and sorrows of life forgotten, and all sorrow and sighing fled away—excepting grief for past sins, remaining corruption, and that Christ is not

---

[129] Colossians 2:2

loved more, and God is not honored more in this world. She felt compassionate grief towards fellow creatures—a daily sensible doing and suffering everything for God, for a long time past, eating, working, sleeping, bearing pain and trouble for God, and doing all as the service of love, with a continual uninterrupted cheerfulness, peace, and joy. "Oh how good," she said, "is it to work for God in the day-time and at night to lie down under His smiles!" High experiences and religious affections in her have not been attended with any disposition at all to neglect the necessary business of a secular calling, time in reading and prayer, or other exercises of devotion; but worldly business has been attended with great alacrity[130] as part of the service of God. She said that when she carried out her daily responsibilities as unto the Lord, they were found to be as good as prayer. These things have been accompanied with exceeding concern and zeal for moral duties, and that all professors may with them adorn the doctrine of God their Saviour. She had an uncommon care to perform relative and social duties, and a noted eminence in them. She maintained a great inoffensiveness of life and conversation in the sight of others, as well as a great meekness, gentleness, and benevolence of spirit and behavior. There was a great alteration in those things that formerly used to be the person's failings. She seemed to be much overcome and swallowed up by the late great increase of grace to the observation of those who are most conversant and intimately acquainted with her.

In times of the brightest light and highest flights of love and joy, there was found no disposition to the opinion of being now perfectly free from sin (according to the notion of the Wesleys and their followers, and some other high pretenders to spirituality in

---

[130] Promptness and cheerfulness

these days) but exceedingly the contrary. At such times especially, it was seen how loathsome and polluted her soul really was. Her soul and body, and every act and word, appeared like rottenness and corruption in the pure and holy light of God's glory. She did not slight instruction or means of grace any more for having had great discoveries. On the contrary, she never was more sensible of the need of instruction than now. And one thing more may be added; these things have been attended with a particular dislike of placing religion much in dress, and spending much zeal about those things that in themselves are matters of indifference, or a pretense of humility, or a demure and melancholy countenance, or anything singular and superstitious.

Jonathan's Commentary on
Sarah's Narrative

Now if such things are enthusiasm and the offspring of a distempered brain, then let my brain be possessed evermore of that happy distemper! If this be distraction, I pray God that the world of mankind may all be seized with this benign, meek, beneficent, beatific, glorious distraction! . . . What notion have they of true religion who reject what has here been described? What shall we find to correspond with these expressions of Scripture? "The peace of God that passeth all understanding."[131] "Rejoicing with joy unspeakable and full of glory."[132] "God's shining into our hearts, to give the light of the knowledge of the glory of God in the face of Jesus Christ."[133] "With open face, beholding as in a glass the glory of God, and being changed into the same image, from glory to glory, even as by the Spirit of the Lord."[134] "Being called out of darkness into marvelous light."[135] "Having the day-star arise in our hearts."[136] What, let me ask, if these things that have been mentioned do not correspond with these expressions? What else can we find that does correspond with them?"

---

[131] Philippians 4:7
[132] I Peter 1:8
[133] II Corinthians 4:6
[134] II Corinthians 3:18
[135] I Peter 2:9
[136] II Peter 1:19

Sereno's Commentary on Jonathan's Edition of Sarah's Narrative

Mr. Edwards adds that he had witnessed many instances, in Northampton and elsewhere, of other persons which were in general of the same kind [as Mrs. Edwards] though not so high in degree in any instance. Many of them were not so pure and unmixed or so well regulated. In some individuals who discovered very intense religious affections there was obviously a great mixture of nature with grace, and in some a sad degenerating of religious affections; yet in most instances, they were uniform in their character and obviously the result of fervent piety.

That such full and clear discoveries of the divine excellency and glory as those recited in the preceding narrative are uncommon, is unhappily too true. Still, they are far from being singular, for accounts of a similar nature may be found in the private diaries of men of distinguished piety in almost every age of the church. They are not, however, probably more uncommon than are great attainments in piety, and when enjoyed by those who have made such attainments, ought in no respect to be regarded as surprising. There is certainly in God a goodness and a glory infinitely surpassing the comprehension of the highest created beings. This goodness and glory, which constitutes the divine beauty and loveliness of God, are able to reveal [God] to the mind of every intelligent creature as far as his faculties extend. If the mind, to which this revelation is made, has a supreme relish for holiness, the discovery of this spiritual beauty of the divine mind will communicate to it an enjoyment which is pure and heavenly in its nature. And the degree of this enjoyment, in every case, will be

105

proportioned to the measure of the faculties and to the fullness of the discovery. This is obviously true in the heavenly world. God there reveals His glory—not in all its infinite brightness—this He cannot do to a created intelligence. He reveals it, however, in as strong an effulgence as the minds of saints and angels can endure. Were a revelation equally clear and full to be made to one of us here on earth, it would obviously overwhelm and destroy the life of the body. For John, even when he beheld the glorified body of Christ, fell at His feet as dead. In proportion as an individual is possessed of holiness, so much more near does he come to God, and so much more clear and distinct is his perception of His true character. "If a man loves me," says Christ, "he will keep my words; and my Father will love him, and we will come unto him, and make our abode with him."[137] Such discoveries of the divine beauty and glory are therefore the promised reward as well as the natural consequence of distinguished holiness, and they are a well authenticated narrative of the manner in which they were made in a given instance, even if they were unusual in degree. Instead of exciting our distrust or surprise, they should lead us, with a noble emulation, to "press forward towards the mark, for the prize of the high calling of God in Christ Jesus."[138]

---

[137] John 14:23
[138] Philippians 3:14

The increased revelation of Christ in His beauty and worth was not reserved for Sarah alone—it is a gift that God has purchased for all of His children. The same blood and righteousness that covered Sarah covers everyone who repents of their sins and trusts in Him. Christ's righteous life and death sufficiently paid the price to bring *every* saint directly to the throne of God. In Christ, the saints are not only forgiven, declared righteous, and reconciled to God, but they are actually embraced into His bosom as beloved sons and daughters!

Ephesians 1:3 says, "Blessed be the God and Father of our Lord Jesus Christ, who has blessed us with every spiritual blessing in the heavenly places in Christ." What does it mean to be blessed with every spiritual blessing? It means that all of the love that the Father has for the Son—the Son of His bosom, the Son of His image, the Son in whom He has had inexplicable delight for all eternity—all of that love He now lavishes upon those who are in His Son! It is as if the saints swim under the waterfall of the love the Father for the Son and are completely saturated in His Fatherly delights and affections.

Sarah swam deeper in His love than most—but the ability to swim is given to all who are in Christ—He purchased it with His blood. The question is: how deep will we swim? Will we trust the Spirit as He escorts us down into the depths of the sea of love, to show us the glorious, hidden treasures of the knowledge of God in Christ that lay buried for His children to discover and enjoy? Christ's righteous life and atoning death ensure passage for all believers. However, it requires leaving the safety of the shallow waters. It often demands being willing to swim through dark waters, turbulent waters, dangerous waters, and lonely waters— yet the reward of swimming through this subterraneous sea is the treasure of pure ecstasy and eternal pleasure in God that ravishes the soul and transports it to heights of joy beyond sensory delight and human comprehension.

Let us pray for grace to dive deep into the love of God, by "lay[ing] aside every encumbrance, and the sin which so easily entangles us, and let us run with endurance the race that is set before us, fixing our eyes on Jesus, the author and perfecter of faith, who for the joy set before Him endured the cross, despising the shame, and has sat down at the right hand of the throne of God."[139] Let us turn away from creature-comforts and the things of this world, that we might receive the greater comfort in the "Comforter" who has come.

Scripture holds out wonderful promises for those who pant and thirst, yea "faint" and "dive" after God. He will come to them and they will behold Him! There can be no greater gift or pleasure![140] Therefore, "Let us know, let us press on to know the Lord. His going forth [toward us!] is as certain as the dawn; and *He will come to us* like the rain, like the spring rain watering the earth.[141] For, "The Lord longs to be gracious to you, and therefore He waits on high to have compassion on you. For the Lord is a God of justice; how blessed are all those who long for Him!"[142] Behold, He "stands at the door and knocks; if anyone hears [His] voice and opens the door, [He] will come in to him and will dine

---

[139] Hebrews 12:1-2
[140] "In Thy presence is fullness of joy, in Thy right hand are pleasures forevermore." Psalm 16:11
[141] Hosea 6:3
[142] Isaiah 30:18

with him and he with [the Lord].[143] O beloved of the Lord, open to Him,[144] "eat, drink and imbibe deeply"[145] of His love.

[143] Revelation 3:20; see also Song of Solomon 5:2, "A voice! My beloved was knocking; 'Open to me, my sister, my darling, my perfect one'. "
[144] Song of Solomon 5:2; Psalm 81:10
[145] Song of Solomon 5:2

Section III

The Narrative of Phebe

The narrative of Phebe testifies to the work of God in a four-year-old girl. It is recorded by her pastor, Jonathan Edwards, who believed she was truly converted. It serves as an illustration of what saving faith looks like in a young child. Phebe's desire for the presence of God in prayer, her love for the preaching of His Word, her sincere sorrow, repentance, and repulsion over sin, and her intercession for lost family members are the fruit of a heart that savingly believes. Her testimony is an encouragement of what God can do in a young child and a reminder that the fruit of saving faith, though varying in degree, is the same in both young and old.

Introduction by Mary Bethany Adams

Phebe was devoted to God. She loved Him more than anyone else. She fulfilled the verse, "When you pray, go into your inner room, and when you have shut your door, pray to your Father who is in secret, and your Father who sees in secret will repay you."[146] She set a wonderful example for us in prayer. She was often found alone, crying out to God and worshiping Him. She was truly sorry when she disobeyed and was quick to repent. She loved His people and the preaching of His Word. She labored in prayer for her lost family members, asking God to save them. The Spirit of God did this work in her, and it is a beautiful picture of His saving grace.

---

[146] Matthew 6:6

111

The Narrative of Phebe by Jonathan Edwards

Phebe was born in March, 1731. At about the end of April, or the beginning of May, in the year 1735, when she was about four-years-old, she was greatly affected by the talk of her brother, who was hopefully converted at the age of eleven. After his conversion, he began to talk earnestly with Phebe about religion. Her parents did not know of it at that time and had not spoken to her about religion themselves, supposing her to be too young to understand. But after her brother had talked with her, they observed that she began to listen very carefully to the instruction they gave the older children. Moreover, she was observed to go to her closet, several times a day, for secret prayer. She grew more and more engaged in religion, and was more frequent in her closet, till at last she was found praying five or six times a day. She was so engaged in prayer that nothing would divert her from it. Her mother mentioned some very remarkable instances.

Once, of her own accord, Phebe said that she was not able to find God. But on Thursday, the last day of July, about the middle of the day, being in the closet, her mother heard her speaking aloud. She was very importunate and engaged in prayer. Her mother could distinctly hear her cry out with extraordinary earnestness and distress of soul, "Blessed Lord, give me salvation! I pray, beg, pardon all my sins." When the child finished, she came out of the closet, sat down by her mother and cried out loud. Her mother asked her several times why she was crying, but she did not answer. She continued crying and writhing her body to and fro, like one in anguish of spirit. Her mother asked her whether she was afraid that God would not give her salvation. She answered, "Yes, I am afraid I shall go to hell!" Her mother endeavored to quiet her and told her not to cry. She said that she

112

must be a good girl and pray every day and that she hoped God would give her salvation sometime soon.

But this did not quiet her at all. She continued crying, till at length she ceased, smiled, and said, "Mother, the Kingdom of Heaven is come to me!" Her mother was surprised at her sudden alteration of speech. The child presently spoke again and said, "There is another come to me, and there is another, there is three." Being asked what she meant, she answered, "One is, 'Thy will be done,'[147] and there is another, 'Enjoy Him forever.'"[148] When the child said, "There is three come to me," she referred to three passages of her catechism that came to her mind.

After she had said this, she retired again into her closet for prayer. Then, after some time passed, she came out of her closet and cheerfully told her mother, "I can find God now! I love God!" Her mother asked her how well she loved God, whether she loved God better than her father and mother, and she said, "Yes." She asked her whether she loved God better than her little sister, Rachel. She answered, "Yes, better than anything!"

Then her elder sister asked her where she could find God. She answered, "In heaven." Her sister replied, "Have you been in heaven?" "No," answered Phebe. By this, it seems, that she did not see God with the eyes of her body, but with the eyes of her heart. Her mother asked her whether she was afraid of going to hell. She answered, "Yes, I was; but now I am not." Her mother asked her whether she thought that God had given her salvation. She answered, "Yes." Her mother asked her when. She answered,

---

[147] This is the answer to question 103 of the Westminster Shorter Catechism, "What do we pray for in the third petition [of the Lord's prayer]?" Answer: "Thy will be done ..."

[148] This is the answer to the first question of the Westminster Shorter Catechism, "What is the chief end of man?" Answer: "To glorify God and enjoy Him forever."

"Today." She appeared all that afternoon exceedingly cheerful and joyful. That evening, as she lay in bed, she asked one of her little cousins to come to her. When he came she said, "Heaven is better than earth." The next day, her mother asked her why God made her. She answered, "To serve Him," and added, "Everybody should serve God and get an interest in Christ."

That same day the older children seemed much affected with the extraordinary change in Phebe. Her sister, Abigail, took occasion to counsel her, on which Phebe burst out in tears and said, "Poor Nabby." Her mother told her not to cry because she hoped that God would give Nabby salvation, but that did not quiet her. She continued crying for some time. When she had in a measure ceased, she saw her sister Eunice beside her, and she burst out again, "Poor Eunice!" When she was almost done, she went into another room, and there looked upon her sister Naomi, and burst out again, crying, "Poor Amy!" Her mother was greatly affected at such behavior in a child and knew not what to say to her. When asked why she was crying, she said, "I am afraid they will go to hell."

At night, a certain minister spoke with her about the Lord. After he left, she leaned on the table with tears running from her eyes. When she was asked why she was crying, she said, "I was thinking about God." The next day, she was in a very affectionate frame. She had four turns of crying and then endeavored to curb herself and hide her tears. On the Sabbath,[149] she was asked whether she believed in God, and she answered, "Yes." When someone said to her that Christ was the Son of God, she answered, "I know."

---

[149] i.e., Sunday, the Lord's Day

From this time, there appeared to be a very remarkable change in the child. She was very careful to keep the Lord's Day and seemed to long for it before it even came. She would often ask during the week how many more days until the Sabbath-day. She seemed to love God's house and was very eager to go there. Her mother once asked her why she wanted to go to church, whether it was just to see her friends. She said, "No, I want to hear Mr. Edwards preach." When she was in the place of worship, she did not spend her time there as the other children but listened with an attention that is very extraordinary for such a young child. She also appeared very desirous to go to private religious meetings. She was still and attentive during family prayer. She seemed to delight in hearing religious conversation. One time, after I had the occasion to speak with her about the Lord, she looked out the window very wistfully as my companions and I left her house and said, "I wish they would come to our house again!" Her mother asked her why she said this. She said, "I love to hear them talk."

She seemed to fear God and have an extraordinary dread of sinning against Him. Her mother mentioned the following instance. Sometime in August, last year, she went with the older children to pick plums from the neighbor's tree, not knowing it was wrong. When she brought some of the plums home, her mother mildly reproved her and told her that she must not take plums without permission because it was stealing. The child seemed greatly surprised and burst into tears, "I won't have these plums!" Turning to her sister Eunice, she very earnestly said to her, "Why did you ask me to go to that plum tree?" The other children did not seem to be much affected or concerned, but there was no pacifying Phebe. Her mother told her that she would go and ask the neighbor if the children could eat the plums and that if the neighbor said "yes," it would not be sin for her to eat them.

When her mother returned, she told her that the neighbor had given permission for the children to eat the plums, so now she might eat them, and it would not be sin. This stilled her a little while, but then she broke out again into an exceeding fit of crying. Her mother asked her why she was crying since she had permission to eat the plums. She replied, "It is because it is sin." She continued a considerable time crying and said that she would not go again to the neighbor's plum tree even if Eunice asked her a hundred times. She retained an aversion to plums for a considerable time under the remembrance of her former sin.

Sometimes Phebe appeared greatly affected and delighted with certain texts of Scripture. Particularly, about the beginning of November, the text that came to her mind was Revelation 3:20, "Behold, I stand at the door, and knock: If any man hears My voice, and open the door, I will come in, and sup with him, and he with Me." She spoke of it to her family with an appearance of joy, a smiling countenance, and an elevation of voice. Afterward, she went into another room where her mother overheard her talking very earnestly to the other children about this verse. She heard her say with an air of exceeding joy and admiration, "Why this verse means to sup[150] with God."

In about the middle of winter, very late in the night, when all were asleep, her mother heard her weeping. The next morning, her mother asked her if she was crying last night. The child answered, "Yes, I did cry a little, for I was thinking about God and Christ, and that they loved me."

She has often manifested a great concern for the good of others' souls and has been seen many times to be giving affectionate counsel to the other children. Once, about the latter

---

[150] i.e., commune with

end of September, Phebe and some other children were in a room by themselves husking Indian corn. Then Phebe came out and sat by the fire. Her mother noticed that she appeared to have a more serious and pensive countenance than usual. At last, she broke the silence and said, "I have been talking to Nabby and Eunice." Her mother asked her what she had said to them. She answered, "I told them they must pray and prepare to die; that they had but a little while to live in this world, and they must be always ready." At other times, Phebe took the opportunity to talk to the other children about their souls, and the children seemed to be greatly affected by her. She was once exceeding importunate with her mother to pray with her sister, Naomi. Her mother endeavored to put her off, but she pulled her by the sleeve and seemed as if she would by no means be denied. At last her mother told her, "Amy must go and pray by herself." "But," said Phebe, "she will not go," and pleaded that her mother go with her.

She had an uncommon spirit of charity, particularly on the following occasion. A poor man was visiting their house and told them of the difficulties he was reduced to by having lost his cow. She took much notice of it and was wrought exceedingly with compassion. After she had attentively listened to him, she went away to her father, who was in the shop, and entreated him to give that man one of their cows. She told him, "The poor man has no cow!" Her father told her that they could not spare one of their cows. Then she entreated her father to let the poor man and his family come live in their house. She had much more talk of the same nature, whereby she manifested bowels of compassion to the poor.

She has manifested great love to her minister, particularly when I returned from my long journey last fall. When she heard of it, she appeared very joyful at the news, and told the children of it,

117

with an elevated voice, as the most joyful of tidings, repeating it over and over, "Mr. Edwards is come home! Mr. Edwards is come home!"

She continued in secret prayer and seemed to have no desire that others should observe her, being a child of a reserved temper. Every night, before she went to bed, she would say her catechism. She never forgot to say it but once, and then, after she was asleep, she thought of it and cried out in tears, "I didn't say my catechism!" She would not be quieted till her mother asked her the catechism as she lay in bed. She sometimes appeared to be in doubt about the condition of her soul, and when asked whether she thought she was prepared for death, she spoke something doubtfully about it. At other times she seemed to have no doubt, but when asked, replied, "Yes," without hesitation.

The Life of Jonathan's Sister, Jerusha

Sarah was pregnant with her second child when Jonathan's sister, Jerusha, died. Jonathan and Sarah named their daughter Jerusha in honor of his sister. Below is a brief biographical sketch of Jonathan's sister, Jerusha, with the prayer that it will encourage young readers to follow in her steps.

Jonathan's Sister, Jerusha Edwards

Jerusha was born in June 1710, and on the testimony of a friend, was a young lady of great sweetness of temper, of a fine understanding, and of a beautiful countenance. She was devoted to reading from childhood, and though fond of books of taste and amusement, she customarily preferred those which require close thought and are fitted to strengthen and inform the mind. Like her sisters, she had received a thorough education, both English and classical, and by her proficiency, had justified the views of her father and sustained the honor and claims of her sex. In conversation, she was solid and instructive beyond her years, yet at the same time, was sprightly and active, and had an uncommon share of native wit and humor. Her wit was always delicate and kind and used merely for recreation. According to the rule she prescribed to another, it constituted "the sauce, and not the food, in the entertainment." Being fond of retirement and meditation from early life, she passed much of her leisure time in solitary walks in the groves behind her father's house; and the richness of her mind, in moral reflection and philosophical remark, proved that these hours were not wasted in reverie but occupied by solid thought and profitable contemplation. Habitually serene and cheerful, she was contented and happy; not envious of others, not desirous of admiration, not ambitious nor aspiring; and while she valued highly the esteem of her friends and of the wise and good, she was firmly convinced that her happiness depended chiefly and ultimately on the state of her own mind. She appeared to have gained the entire government of her temper and passions, discovered uncommon equanimity and firmness under trials, and while in difficult cases she sought the best advice yet ultimately acted for herself. Her religious life began in childhood; and from that time, meditation, prayer, and reading the sacred Scriptures were not a prescribed task but a coveted enjoyment. Her sisters, who knew how much of her time she daily passed alone, had the best reason to believe that no place was so pleasant to her as her own retirement and no society so delightful as solitude with God. She read theology as a science, with the deepest interest, and pursued the systematic study of the Scriptures by the help of the best commentaries. Her observance of the Sabbath was exemplary in solemnly preparing for it, in allotting to it the prescribed hours, and in devoting it only to sacred employments; and in the solemn and entire devotion of her mind to the duties of the sanctuary, she appeared habitually to feel with David, "Holiness becometh Thine house forever."[151] Few persons attend more closely to preaching or judge more correctly concerning it, or have higher pleasure in that which is solid, pungent, and practical. She saw and conversed with God in His works of creation and providence. Her religious joy was, at times, intense and elevated. After telling one of her sisters on a particular occasion that she could not describe it, she observed to her that it seemed like a streak of light shining in a dark place; and reminded her of a line from Watts's Lyrics, "And sudden, from the clearing skies, a gleam of glory broke."

---

[151] Psalm 93:5

Her conscience was truly enlightened and her conduct appeared to be governed by principle. She approved of the best things and discovered great reverence for religion and strong attachment to the truly pious and conscientious; she was severe in her estimate of herself and charitable in judging of others; she was not easily provoked and usually tried to excuse the provocation; she was unapt to cherish prejudices and lamented and strove to conceal the faults of Christians.

On the testimony of those who knew her best, "She was a remarkably loving, dutiful, obedient daughter and a very kind and loving sister," "very helpful and serviceable in the family and willingly laboring with her own hands," "kind and friendly to her neighbors," attentive to the sick, charitable to the poor, prone to sympathize with the afflicted, and merciful to the brutes; and at the same time, respectful to superiors, obliging to equals, condescending and affable to inferiors, and manifesting sincere good will to all mankind. Courteous and easy in her manners, she was also modest, unostentatious, and retiring; and while she uniformly respected herself, she commanded the respect of all who saw her. She was fond of all that was comely in dress but averse to everything happy and gaudy. She loved peace and strove to reconcile those who were at variance; she was delicately attentive to those of her sex who were slighted by others; she received reproofs with meekness and told others of their faults with so much sweetness and faithfulness as to increase their esteem and affection for herself. She detested all guile, and management, and deception, all flattery and falsehood, and wholly refused to associate with those who exhibited this character. She was most careful and select in her friendships and most true and faithful to her friends—highly valuing their affection and discovering the deepest interest in their welfare. Her conversation and conduct indicated uncommon innocence and purity of mind, and she avoided many things which are thought correct by multitudes who are strictly virtuous. During her sickness, she was not forsaken. A day or two before its termination, she manifested a remarkable admiration of the grace and mercy of God through Jesus Christ to sinners, and particularly to herself, saying, "It is wonderful, it surprises me." A part of the time she was in some degree delirious; but, when her mind wandered, it seemed to wander heavenward. Just before her death, she attempted to sing a hymn, entitled, "The Absence of Christ," and died, in the full possession of her rational powers, expressing her hope of eternal salvation through His blood. This first example of the ravages of death in this numerous family was a most trying event to all its members; and the tenderness with which they cherished the memory of her who was gone probably terminated only with life. The second daughter of Mr. and Mrs. Jonathan Edwards was born on the 16th of the following April, named Jerusha, after his deceased sister.[152]

---

[152] *The Works of Jonathan Edwards,* Vol. 1: lxxxii-lxxxiii.

The Descendants of Jonathan and Sarah Edwards

The following is a copy of the Family Record, in his own hand, in the Family Bible.

Jonathan Edwards, son of Timothy and Esther Edwards of Windsor in Connecticut. I was born Oct. 5, 1703. I was ordained at Northampton, Feb. 15, 1727. I was married to Miss Sarah Pierrepont, July 28, 1727. My wife was born Jan. 9, 1710.

-My daughter **Sarah** was born on a Sabbath day, between 2 and 3 o'clock in the afternoon, Aug. 25, 1728.

-My daughter **Jerusha** was born on a Sabbath day, towards the conclusion of the afternoon exercise, April 26, 1730.

-My daughter **Esther** was born on a Sabbath day, between 9 and 10 o'clock in the forenoon, Feb. 13, 1732.

-My daughter **Mary** was born April 7, 1734, being Sabbath day, the sun being about an hour and a half high, in the morning.

-My daughter **Lucy** was born on Tuesday, the last day of Aug. 1736, between 2 and 3 o'clock in the morning.

-My son **Timothy** was born on Tuesday, July 25, 1738, between 6 and 7 o'clock in the morning.

-My daughter **Susannah** was born on Friday, June 20, 1740, at about 3 in the morning.

-All the family above named had the measles at the latter end of the year 1740.

-My daughter **Eunice** was born on Monday morning, May 9, 1743, about half an hour after midnight, and was baptized the Sabbath following.

-My son **Jonathan** was born on a Sabbath-day night, May 26, 1745, between 9 and 10 o'clock, and was baptized the Sabbath following.

-My daughter Jerusha died on a Sabbath day, Feb. 14, 1747, about 5 o'clock in the morning, aged 17.

-My daughter **Elizabeth** was born on Wednesday, May 6, 1747, between 10 and 11 o'clock at night, and was baptized the Sabbath following.

-My son **Pierrepont** was born on a Sabbath-day night, April 8, 1750, between 8 and 9 o'clock; and was baptized the Sabbath following.

-I was dismissed from my pastoral relation to the first church in Northampton, June 22, 1750.

-My daughter Sarah was married to Mr. Elihu Parsons, June 11, 1750.

-My daughter Mary was married to Timothy Dwight, Esq. of Northampton, Nov. 8, 1750.

-My daughter Esther was married to the Rev. Aaron Burr of Newark, June 29, 1752.

-I was properly initiated President of New Jersey College, by taking the previous oaths, Feb. 16, 1758.

The following was added by family members after his death:

-Rev. Jonathan Edwards died of smallpox, March 22, 1758, and was buried March 24th.

-Esther Edwards Burr, wife of Rev. Aaron Burr, died at Princeton, April 7, 1758, of a short illness, aged 26.

-Sarah Edwards, wife of Jonathan Edwards, died Oct. 2, 1758, about 12 o'clock, and was buried at Princeton the day following.

-Elizabeth Edwards, daughter of Jonathan and Sarah, died at Northampton, Jan. 1. 1762, aged 14.

-Lucy Edwards Woodbridge died at Stockbridge in Oct. 1786, aged 50.

-Rev. Jonathan Edwards, D.D. died at Schenectady, Aug. 1. 1801, aged 56.

-Susannah Edwards Porter died at Hadley, in the spring of 1802, aged 61.

-Sarah Edwards Parsons died at Goshen, Mass. May 15, 1805, aged 76.

-Mary Edwards Dwight died at Northampton, Feb. 1807, aged 72.

-Timothy Edwards died at Stockbridge in the autumn of 1813, aged 75.

-Eunice Edwards Hunt died at Newburn, N.C. in the autumn of 1822, aged 79.

-Pierrepont Edwards died at Bridgeport, April 14, 1826, aged 76.[153]

---

[153] *The Works of Jonathan Edwards,* Vol. 1: cclxxiv.

Made in the USA
San Bernardino, CA
10 July 2016